"Mike Aquilina has an extraordinary gift for bringing the events and personalities of early Christianity alive. That is fortunate for us, since the era of which he writes so well is a rich source of enlightenment concerning the roots of faith as well as a model by which to measure our own living of the Gospel. In *The Eucharist Foretold: The Lost Prophecy of Malachi* he tells the fascinating story of how a Eucharistic prophecy from the Old Testament inspired Christians to find in the Holy Sacrifice a source of unity and vitality in troubled times just as we can and should do today."

RUSSELL SHAW
Author of *American Church* and other books

"Mike Aquilina has written on a subject long overlooked. This is a clear prophecy of the Eucharist for Catholics, Orthodox, and apostolic tradition Christians. Thank you, Mike, for a new look at this forgotten prophecy from the Hebrew Bible that foretells the Eucharistic sacrifice of Christians."

JOHN MICHAEL TALBOT
Founder, Spiritual Father, and General Minister of the Brothers and Sisters of Charity,
Little Portion Hermitage

"When it comes to expounding on the early Fathers of the Church, few can match the scholarly expertise, the literary flair, and the imaginative presentation of Mike Aquilina. *The Eucharist Foretold* is a perfect example. Taking Malachi's prophecy that God would be worshiped from the rising of the sun to its setting, Aquilina marvelously shows that the Fathers celebrated, in wonder, that this prophesy was being fulfilled in their day—the Mass was extending to the farthest limits of the sea. That the sun never sets on the celebration of the Eucharist is indeed a cause for rejoicing, not only for the Fathers, but also for us—our world is much bigger than was theirs."

THOMAS G. WEINANDY, OFM, CAP.
Member of the Vatican's International
Theological Commission

"*The Eucharist Foretold* grabs your attention from the very first line. Mike Aquilina captures your imagination with the sun never setting on the celebration of the Mass, and then applies that universal view to the history of salvation, from Malachi to this day. For those who hunger for Christ in the Holy Eucharist, who know as Pope Benedict taught that the Eucharist is the event at the center of absolutely everything, you have to read this book."

REV. FRANCIS J. HOFFMAN, J.C.D.
Executive Director/CEO, Relevant Radio

"Salvation history is high drama, and few people are capable of communicating that with as much wit, zeal, and obvious love for the material as Mike Aquilina. Drawing from early Christian sources, liturgical texts, and Jewish scholarship, Mike does a masterful job of shedding light on one of the most mysterious and intriguing Eucharistic prophecies of the Old Testament. I was hooked from the first paragraph."

MATT SWAIM
Host of The SonRise Morning Show,
EWTN Radio

"It's prayed at Mass all day and all over the world: '. . . You never cease to gather a people to yourself, so that from rising of the sun to its setting, a pure sacrifice may be offered to your name.' Many Catholics probably have no idea that those words in the Third Eucharistic Prayer come from the last prophet of the Old Testament. Don't believe that God had the Eucharist in mind all along? Read this book. In his usual accessible style, Mike Aquilina shows us how the earliest Christians understood that the Prophet Malachi, at the cusp of the New Testament, prepared us for the institution of the Eucharist as the 'pure sacrifice' that could not be accomplished by any of God's people, but only by God himself. This book is for anyone who wants a deeper understanding of the Eucharist and of our participation in that sacrifice—which should be everyone!"

ANNA MITCHELL
Producer and co-host of the SonRise
Morning Show, EWTN Radio

"Mike Aquilina hits another home run! No one makes the Early Christian authors more accessible than Mike does. In these difficult times it is so strengthening to have the perspective that Mike provides for both scholar and layman. The church has been through a lot, and her Lord has never left Her. Well done once again!"

FR. RICHARD SIMON
Pastor of St. Lambert Parish, Skokie, IL,
and host of Fr. Simon Says, Relevant Radio

THE
EUCHARIST
FORETOLD

THE EUCHARIST FORETOLD

THE LOST PROPHECY OF MALACHI

MIKE AQUILINA

EMMAUS ROAD
PUBLISHING

Steubenville, Ohio
www.emmausroad.org

Emmaus Road Publishing
1468 Parkview Circle
Steubenville, Ohio 43952

Library of Congress Control Number: 2019948950
ISBN: 978-1-64585-003-8

Cover design and layout by Emily Feldkamp
Cover Image: Habakkuk 2:1–15. In Sanders, Henry Arthur. *Facsimile of the Washington Manuscript of the Minor Prophets in the Freer Collection and the Berlin Fragment of Genesis.* Ann Arbor, MI: University of Michigan, 1927.

For my brother Charlie

Contents

ACKNOWLEDGMENTS

I NEED TO THANK the folks at Emmaus Road Publishing, especially Chris Erickson and Rob Corzine, for their patience and encouragement as I took way too long to produce this book. I'm typing this page one hour before my extended deadline.

Kevin Knight (NewAdvent.org) and Roger Pearse (Tertullian.org) generously allowed me to use and adapt their e-texts for this book. Most of the texts I quote are from the nineteenth-century translations published in three series: The Apostolic Fathers (edited by J. B. Lightfoot), The Ante-Nicene Fathers, and The Nicene and Post-Nicene Fathers. The English language has undergone major changes since these were published. So I have taken the liberty of updating the translations, after consulting other translations and, whenever possible, the texts in the original languages.

My friend Chris Bailey generously provided me with new translations for my modern French and Italian sources, as well as for some passages in the Apostolic Fathers.

Prologue

THE NEW DAY DAWNS FIRST ON KIRIBATI. It has to start somewhere, and the International Date Line makes a sudden dodge to the east to avoid slicing this sprawling chain of coral atolls in two with the blade of the calendar. It's a country with a Catholic majority, and as the first rays of sunlight gild the tops of the coconut palms, morning Mass is already under way.

As the earth keeps turning, the sun is soon rising over the great metropolis of Manila, capital of the Philippines. It's a city of thirteen million already in the grip of its Sunday-morning rush. Horns are honking; people are pouring into buses; bicycles are weaving in and out of traffic; wildly colorful jitneys are roving the streets. But in the great Cathedral, the sounds of the city are a forgotten undertone as the host is elevated. Since the 1500s, this has been a city where Catholics gather in great numbers for the sacrifice of the Eucharist.

Still the sunlight advances around the globe, and now it's bright mid-morning in Kerala, where—if we believe the universal tradition of the local church and the ancient writers—the apostle Thomas planted the church that still flourishes here today. In this place the ancient liturgy continues to bring in crowds of believers who proudly call themselves

Thomas Christians. They have been meeting for the sacrifice of the Mass since long before there was a France or a Germany or an England, and their Mass is steeped in local color. But it's the same sacrifice, the same Eucharist that goes back to Christ in an uninterrupted line.

Soon, as the light pours westward, it's noon in Jerusalem, the city where Christ walked and preached and died and rose again, where churches mark all the important sites associated with his last days before his sacrifice on the cross. And here, where Christ himself offered the first Eucharist, that same Eucharist is still offered before pilgrims from every nation under the sun.

In Rome, the Eternal City, the pope is saying Mass in St. Peter's Basilica, the largest and most magnificent church in the Christian world. Rich vestments, expensive incense, and an enormous choir are there to make the occasion an impressive spectacle. But meanwhile, the Mass is also going on in an out-of-the-way suburban parish where the faithful poor gather. The vestments aren't as rich, and the congregation will have to do its own singing today. But the miracle is the same. On both altars, the sacrifice of Christ on the cross is made present to the worshipers in that particular place and at that particular time, because it is everywhere and for all time.

Light washes over Africa, and we pay a flying visit to Lagos in Nigeria, a country of many religions, but one where the Christian faith has such a strong presence that the region produces surplus priests for export. Here the liturgy is a beautiful spectacle of splendid colors and robust African harmonies. But it's the same Mass, the same sacrifice of the Eucharist.

The day grows older, and across the Atlantic, afternoon Mass is being celebrated in the beautiful old city of Salvador de Bahia in Brazil. Since the Portuguese settled the Brazilian coast, the faithful have gathered for Mass. The congregation here is a wonderfully diverse mixture of people whose ancestors were native Brazilian, African, Portuguese, Japanese, Italian, German, and from every other corner of the globe.

We continue westward, and it's time for late-afternoon Masses in Pittsburgh, a city whose mighty industries lured immigrants from all over Europe. Even today you can occasionally hear the liturgy in Polish or Italian or Ukrainian or Croatian—or any of a dozen other traditional languages. But it's the same sacrifice, and the same Church that offers it.

And finally, as the day comes to an end, we visit French Polynesia, where once again we're in the land of tropical breezes and coconut palms waving in them. As the sun sets for the last time on today, evening Mass is already being said. It's tomorrow in Kiribati, and the whole cycle is on its way around the world again.

> For from the rising of the sun to its setting my name is great among the nations, and in every place incense is offered to my name, and a pure offering; for my name is great among the nations, says the LORD of hosts. (Mal 1:11)

Whenever the early Christians talked about the Mass, that prophecy from Malachi was sure to come up. The Mass, they believed, was its obvious fulfillment. And our trip around the world seems to be a perfect picture of what the prophet Malachi was talking about. In every nation, from the rising of the sun to its setting, the Mass is offered. It's in hundreds of different languages, with different music, different costumes, different customs—but always the same sacrifice, always the same "pure offering."

We're living in that world Malachi saw in his vision. The nations—the Gentiles—are offering sacrifices to the God of Israel all over the world.

But Malachi's prophecy comes in a very specific context. God is rejecting the offerings of the Temple priests in Jerusalem because (the prophet says) they've been offering damaged goods. The pure offering that the nations are making is contrasted with the polluted offering the priests in Jerusalem are making. Israel and the nations around her are worshiping the same God at last, but they're not together. Here's that verse from Malachi in its context:

> Oh, that there were one among you who would shut the doors, that you might not kindle fire upon my altar in vain! I have no pleasure in you, says the LORD of hosts, and I will not accept an offering from your hand. For from the rising of the sun to its setting my name is great among the nations, and in every place incense is offered to my name, and a pure offering; for my name is great among the nations, says the LORD of hosts. But you profane it when you say that the Lord's table is polluted, and the food for it may be despised. (Mal 1:10–12)

In the same vision Malachi sees the whole world worshiping God with a pure offering, and the doors of the Temple in Jerusalem shut.

And, as we know, the doors of that Temple are no longer open. In fact, there are no doors, because the Romans destroyed the whole building in AD 70.

Traditionally, Christians have looked at that prophecy of Malachi as foretelling the end of the Temple as well as the beginning of the celebration of the Eucharist. They've also often seen it as a prediction that the Christian Church would replace the Jewish religion. Jews, on the other hand, have frequently interpreted Malachi's pure offering as the prayers offered by the Jews scattered throughout the world.

So where does that leave us?

Salvation has come to the Gentiles—and it has come through Israel. But there has also been a parting of the ways. There are Christians and there are Jews, and they worship the same God, but each side thinks the other is wrong.

That's what our story is about. On the one hand, it's the triumphant tale of how Malachi's vision came gloriously true, probably more gloriously than he could have imagined, with offerings made to his God in nations he couldn't possibly have heard of. On the other hand, it's the tragic account of the parting of the ways that we're still living with, the separation of Jews and Christians that broke Paul's heart.

> For I could wish that I myself were accursed and cut off from Christ for the sake of my brethren, my kinsmen by race. They are Israelites, and to them belong the sonship, the glory, the covenants, the giving of the law, the worship, and the promises; to them belong the patriarchs, and of their race, according to the flesh, is the Christ. (Rom 9:3–5)

The triumph and the tragedy both make our world what it is today. And both were probably inevitable from the time of the earliest Christians. They saw themselves living in the world of Malachi's vision, as well as living through his stern rejection of Jerusalem's sacrificial cult. These Christians believed they were the people Malachi spoke of, offering that pure offering from the rising of the sun to its setting. And that was a vision they were willing to die for if necessary.

But even that story of separation isn't all tragedy. If we understand the history behind it, we realize that we aren't really as separate as we think we are. Jews and Christians are one family: that's what makes our arguments so bitter. Nonetheless it's also what gives us hope. We can overcome the centuries of suspicion and hostility on both sides if we understand how the things that separate us are also the things that hold us together.

So let's go back to the days of the early Christians, when it was still illegal to profess the name of Jesus Christ, and let's look at how we got where we are today. We'll see how the Christians rallied around that prophecy of Malachi as their banner, and how they always came back to it as the most effective proof that their faith was the true one.

CHAPTER 1

JUSTIN AND THE PROOF FROM PROPHECY

THE CHARGES HAD BEEN READ, and now the Prefect of Rome—a well-known intellectual by the name of Rusticus—proceeded to the questioning of the accused.

"What kind of life do you live?" he asked, addressing himself to the man who seemed to be the leader of the group.

"Without blame and without condemnation in everyone's opinion," said the accused, who was called Justin. He spoke in Greek: like many easterners resident in Rome, he hardly knew any Latin, and a well-educated official like Rusticus was fluent in Greek.

"What's your philosophy?" Rusticus asked—for the prisoner was dressed in the uniform of a philosopher so that anyone could see he must belong to one of the infinite number of philosophical schools in Rome.

"I have tried to learn all the philosophies," Justin replied. "But I am committed to the true philosophy of the Christians, though it may be distasteful to people with false beliefs."

"This is your preferred philosophy?"

"Yes, because I adopt it on account of faith."

"What do you mean, 'faith'?"

"Our pious faith in the God of the Christians. We believe that he alone was creator of all the world from the beginning. And in the child of God, Jesus Christ, who also was foretold by the prophets as coming to humanity as herald of salvation and teacher of good knowledge. I think what I say is little enough when measured against his infinite Godhead; but I acknowledge the prophetic power, since it was foretold about him whom I just called the Son of God. For you know that in olden days the prophets foretold that he would come among us."

Rusticus was probably thinking, "Blah blah blah," at this point, because he was a philosopher himself, and one who took pride in being a very rational man. He had no time for rubbish about ancient prophecies. So he changed the subject to one of more concern to his administration:

"Where do you assemble?"

"Wherever each one prefers or is able," Justin replied. "Did you really think we could all assemble in one place?"

"Tell me," Rusticus insisted, "where do you assemble? What is the place?"

"As for myself," said Justin, "I live above the baths of Myrtinus, as I have done for the whole of this, my second stay in Rome; and I know of no other place of assembly. As for anyone wanting to come to my place, I would teach him the true philosophy."

"You admit that you are a Christian?" Rusticus asked.

"Yes," Justin replied. "I am a Christian."

And that was really all Rusticus had to hear.

He asked the same question of the others who were

charged with Justin, and they all gave him the same response. Rusticus didn't know much about Christians, and he didn't care to know any more than he did. What he did know was that Christians would refuse to make the legally required sacrifices to the pagan gods, even at the risk of being tortured to death.

It was really quite unreasonable of them. Rusticus was a stoic himself. He believed in one God too, in a vague, rationalistic way. But what harm was there in doing the thing the law prescribed? Just do it and get it over with, and keep your private beliefs to yourself unless you're among people you trust to appreciate them.

As a sensible man, Rusticus was willing to try to reason even with Christians, though he probably didn't expect his rationale to have much effect. "If you are scourged and beheaded," he asked the prisoner in the philosopher's outfit, "do you suppose that you will go up to heaven?"

"I don't just suppose it," said Justin. "I know it for a fact."

"If you do not obey," the prefect warned all the prisoners, "you will be punished."

"We are sure," said Justin, "that we will be saved through our suffering."

Well, there was nothing more to do. You just can't reason with people like that. Rusticus pronounced his judgment, even then leaving the stubborn Christians a way out: "Those who are unwilling to sacrifice to the gods shall be scourged and executed according to the laws." And Rusticus shook his head as he watched Justin and his companions be taken away. They were glorifying God as they went, as if they had just won a victory rather than been condemned to death.

. . . .

Today we know Justin as St. Justin Martyr, and you don't have to be told how he earned his nickname. But his martyrdom is only the end of a remarkable career, and it really isn't even the most interesting thing he did. Though heroic, he was only one of many Christians who died for their faith. However, not many Christians tried to explain Christianity to the outside world in a way philosophers would understand, and that was what Justin set out to do—in fact, he wrote two "Apologies," defenses of the Christian religion against the rumors and charges of the pagans.

Few Christians set out to systematize the Christian argument for Jesus as the Messiah against its Jewish opponents, but Justin took a stab at that too. He wrote a dialogue in which he imagined himself arguing with a Jewish opponent about the prophets in Scripture.

Justin chose the style of dialogue because it was a common form for philosophical treatises. Plato, possibly the most famous of all the Greek philosophers, had written all his important works in the form of dialogues. (Justin certainly was familiar with Plato, since he quotes Plato specifically in his own *Dialogue*.) And it's easy to see why: by putting different ideas in the mouths of different characters, the writer can make his otherwise dull philosophical treatise entertaining as well as enlightening. Furthermore, giving the opponents' arguments as they would come from the mouth of an adversary gave the writer a chance to answer his challengers directly, as if they were standing right in front of him.

Justin easily adopted traditional philosophical forms because he was a philosopher, not just by education but by trade. As he explained to Rusticus, he had learned something of all the common philosophical schools. But he decided he had found truth in only one place—in the Christian Church.

Philosophers in those days offered their teaching services in a marketplace that was always eager to hear new ideas. That was why they wore a particular uniform—a cloak that identified them instantly as philosophers. Well, that and the fact that the uniform gave them instant prestige, like an old-school tie or a Yale sweatshirt.

Justin was intensely proud of being a philosopher, but he recognized that most of the schools of philosophy never got any closer to the truth. If the various disciplines could get to the truth, after all, there wouldn't be an assortment, would there? There would only be the truth.

> In fact philosophy is the greatest possession, and most honorable before God, to whom it leads us and alone commends us; those who have given attention to philosophy are truly holy men. What philosophy is, however, and the reason why it has been sent down to men, have escaped the observation of most; for if this knowledge were one, there would be neither Platonists, nor Stoics, nor Peripatetics, nor Theoretics, nor Pythagoreans.[1]

Justin's explanation for the many schools of philosophy is basically that the followers were more fans than philosophers. They followed some charismatic philosopher and supported his ideas without ever investigating whether those ideas were

---

[1] Justin, *Dialogue with Trypho* 2.

true. And Justin admits that he did the same thing. But over and over he found the experience disappointing.

> At first I wanted to get to know one of these men personally, so I put myself in the hands of a certain Stoic. But after I had spent a considerable time with him, I had not gained any further knowledge of God—for he did not know God himself, and said such instruction was unnecessary.
>
> So I left him and went to another, who was called a Peripatetic [a follower of Aristotle], and thought himself clever. And this man, after having entertained me for the first few days, requested me to settle the fee, in order that our intercourse might not be unprofitable. I therefore abandoned him too, believing him to be no philosopher at all.
>
> But when my soul was eagerly desirous to hear the peculiar and choice philosophy, I came to a very famous Pythagorean—a man who thought much of his own wisdom. And then, when I had an interview with him, willing to become his hearer and disciple, he said, "What then? Are you acquainted with music, astronomy, and geometry? Do you expect to perceive any of those things which conduce to a happy life, if you have not been first informed on those points which wean the soul from sensible objects, and render it fitted for objects which appertain to the mind, so that it can contemplate that which is honorable in its essence and that which is good in its essence?" Having commended many of these branches of learning, and telling me that they were

necessary, he dismissed me when I confessed to him my ignorance. I was rather put out about that, as was to be expected when I failed in my hope, the more so because I thought the man had some knowledge; but thinking again about how long I would have to linger over those branches of learning, I was not able to endure longer procrastination.

In my helpless condition it occurred to me to have a meeting with the Platonists, for their fame was great. I thereupon spent as much of my time as possible with one who had lately settled in our city—a sagacious man, holding a high position among the Platonists. And I progressed, and made the greatest improvements daily. And the perception of immaterial things quite overpowered me, and the contemplation of ideas gave my mind wings, so that in a little while I supposed that I had become wise; and such was my stupidity, I expected forthwith to look upon God, for this is the purpose of Plato's philosophy.[2]

But this was where Justin met an old man on the beach, and his life changed forever. They started to talk; the man asked Justin if he was a philosopher, and of course Justin proudly replied that he was.

However, the man had a question for him: "Does philosophy make happiness?"

Of course it does, Justin replied. Philosophy alone is the knowledge of that which really exists.

But the old man told Justin that, though God really ex-

[2] Justin, *Dialogue with Trypho* 2.

ists, the philosophers have no knowledge of him. In fact his arguments were good enough to make Justin despair of ever knowing anything about God.

Then the old man had a ray of hope for him: there *is* a way to know God. "There existed, long before this time, certain men more ancient than all those who are esteemed philosophers, both righteous and beloved by God, who spoke by the Divine Spirit, and foretold events which would take place, and which are now taking place. They are called prophets." These prophets, the man said, had direct knowledge of God, and the fact that the things they foretold actually happened means that we know we can believe what they tell us. And what they tell us is the truth about God and his Son, Jesus Christ.

Justin never saw the old man again, but he was convinced by that one encounter that he had found the truth he was looking for at last. "I found this philosophy alone to be safe and profitable. Thus, and for this reason, I am a philosopher."

What's fascinating is that the old man had used the argument from prophecy to convince Justin, a pagan philosopher. And it worked—so well, in fact, that Justin would go on to use the same argument in his own writings to the pagans.

These days you'll seldom see Christians using that argument to convince non-Christians: that Jesus must be the Messiah, the Son of God, because the Hebrew prophets predicted his life so accurately. But to Justin it was a very reasonable argument. "Since, then, we prove that everything that has already happened had been predicted by the prophets before it came to pass, we must necessarily believe also that the things that are predicted in the same way, but are yet to come to pass, shall certainly happen."[3]

Justin trusted that the same argument that had convinced him could convince other pagans. Why had it won him over? The fact is that he didn't have the luxury of ignorance that we have. He grew up in Palestine; he *knew* the Jewish writings had been around for ages. If they had long ago foretold things that had actually happened recently, then there must be something more than human about them. You could check up on what the Christians said: the prophets were the proof that Christianity was really true.

And that made Christianity the system for *real* philosophers—that is, lovers of wisdom. That was what made Justin stand out. He didn't give up on philosophy; instead, he believed that in Christianity he had found the only true philosophy. Thus he became one of the first writers to present Christianity as a philosophy as well as a religion.

The description of Christian liturgy that Justin gives is famous because it's one of the earliest thorough accounts. He wrote it in about 150, roughly a century after the liturgical parts of the *Didache*. But what's really striking about Justin's account, as with the shorter *Didache* account, is how little has changed.

How little? In the 1990s, when the Catholic Church was putting together a catechism for the twenty-first century, a panel of the world's foremost experts was assembled for the job. World-class scholars in liturgical practice were working on the project. But they didn't write a new description of the Catholic liturgy. They just picked up Justin's account and ran it verbatim. *Nothing* essential has changed since Justin's time.

[3] Justin, *First Apology* 52.

Here's the whole thing, from Justin's *First Apology*:

But we, after we have thus washed [that is, baptized] the one who has been convinced and has assented to our teaching, bring him to the place where those who are called brethren are assembled, in order that we may offer hearty prayers in common for ourselves and for the enlightened person, and for all others in every place, that we may be counted worthy, now that we have learned the truth, by our works also to be found good citizens and keepers of the commandments, so that we may be saved with an everlasting salvation. Having ended the prayers, we salute one another with a kiss.

There is then brought to the presider of the brethren bread and a cup of wine mixed with water; and he, taking them, gives praise and glory to the Father of the universe, through the name of the Son and of the Holy Spirit, and offers thanks at considerable length for our being counted worthy to receive these things at His hands. And when he has concluded the prayers and thanksgivings, all the people present express their assent by saying "Amen." (This word *Amen* is Hebrew for "so be it.")

And when the presider has given thanks, and all the people have expressed their assent, those we call *deacons* give to each of those present to partake of the bread and wine mixed with water over which the thanksgiving was pronounced, and to those who are absent they carry away a portion.

And among us this food is called the *Eucharist*. No one is allowed to partake of it but one who believes that the things we teach are true, and who has been washed with the washing that is for the remission of sins, and unto regeneration, and who is living the way Christ commanded. For we do not receive these as ordinary bread and ordinary drink. But in the same way Jesus Christ our Savior, having been made flesh by the Word of God, had both flesh and blood for our salvation, so likewise we have been taught that the food which is blessed by the prayer of His word, and from which our blood and flesh by transmutation are nourished, is the flesh and blood of that Jesus who was made flesh. For the apostles, in the memoirs composed by them, which are called Gospels, have thus delivered unto us what was enjoined upon them; that Jesus took bread, and when he had given thanks, said, "Do this in remembrance of me" (Luke 22:19), "this is my body"; and that, after the same manner, having taken the cup and given thanks, he said, "This is my blood," and gave it to them alone. (The wicked devils have imitated this in the mysteries of Mithras, commanding the same thing to be done. For you know, or you can learn, that bread and a cup of water are placed with certain incantations in the mystic rites of one who is being initiated.)

And we afterwards continually remind each other of these things. And the wealthy among us help the needy; and we always keep together; and for all things with which we are supplied, we bless the Maker of all through his Son Jesus Christ, and through the Holy Spirit.

And on the day called Sunday, all who live in cities or in the country gather together to one place, and the memoirs of the apostles or the writings of the prophets are read, as long as time permits; then, when the reader has ceased, the presider verbally instructs, and exhorts to the imitation of these good things. Then we all rise together and pray, and, as we before said, when our prayer is ended, bread and wine and water are brought, and the presider in like manner offers prayers and thanksgivings, according to his ability, and the people assent, saying "Amen"; and there is a distribution to each, and a participation of that over which thanks have been given, and to those who are absent a portion is sent by the deacons. And they who are wealthy, and willing, give what each thinks fit; and what is collected is deposited with the presider, who succors the orphans and widows and those who, through sickness or any other cause, are in want, and those who are in bonds and the strangers sojourning among us, and in a word takes care of all who are in need.

But Sunday is the day on which we all hold our common assembly, because it is the first day on which God, having wrought a change in the darkness and matter, made the world; and Jesus Christ our Savior on the same day rose from the dead. For He was crucified on the day before that of Saturn (Saturday); and on the day after that of Saturn, which is the day of the Sun, having appeared to His apostles and disciples, He taught them these things, which we have submitted to you also for your consideration.[4]

Justin's description of Christian charity is quoted over and over. We love to hear how the early Christians took care of the poor and organized their charitable works. And, of course, that's the point. We know Christians are good people because they're doing good things.

But if we quote Justin's description out of context, we miss its setting. The charity comes in the Mass. Our sacrifices of our own material things are bound up in Jesus' eternal offering of himself.

· · · · · · ·

Justin himself might have felt a particularly close connection with Malachi's prophecy. After all, he himself had come from the rising of the sun (he was raised in Palestine) to the setting (he ended up in Rome).

The idea of Palestine as the rising of the sun and Rome as the setting may have been a common notion in those days. We're used to seeing Rome as the center of the Roman Empire. But to the more ancient civilizations in the East, Rome was a new power that had come out of the far West.

Luke's Acts of the Apostles seems to modern readers to have an abrupt ending: Paul makes it to Rome, and then the story stops. But most commentators see a design in Acts that might have been obvious to the Greek hearers of Luke's time. It's set up in the first chapter: Jesus, just before his as-

---

[4] Justin, *First Apology* 65–67.

cension, tells his disciples, "But you shall be my witnesses in Jerusalem and in all Judea and Samar'ia and to the end of the earth" (Acts 1:8). Indeed, the beginning of the story is confined to Jerusalem; then it spreads to all Judea and Samaria when the infant Church is scattered by the persecution that followed the martyrdom of Stephen. After that, Paul heads westward, until at last he reaches Rome—the "end of the earth." Looked at this way, the ending isn't abrupt at all: it's what we expected from the moment we heard chapter 1.

· · · · · · ·

Justin's *Dialogue with Trypho, a Jew,* is a kind of distilled version of the argument Christians and Jews were having all over the Mediterranean world. First of all, it's a friendly argument. Not that Justin doesn't press his points hard—and, of course, since he's writing the dialogue for both of them, he gets to make some pretty good points. But the whole form of the dialogue presumes that a Christian and a Jew can sit down for quite a long while and argue about their differences without being at each other's throats.

And that argument is based on principles they both understand. They're arguing from Scripture and prophecy. The subject of the debate is simply this: which group is the true Israel?

It was a vital question. In the mind of any outside observer, the most telling accusation against the Christians was that they were something new. Now, the Jewish religion was strange to Romans, but no matter how strange it was, it was ancient. Its age gave it authority. Josephus wrote his famous *Antiquities of the Jews* specifically to show the Roman world that the Jews were an ancient people, and therefore their traditions had value.

Three times in the *Dialogue* Justin quotes Malachi 1:11–12 directly, and he alludes to those two verses at least four more times.[5] Obviously this text is a big deal for him. If Christians *aren't* the true heirs of Israel, then how could Malachi have foreseen their practice so confidently?

> Thus God, anticipating all the sacrifices we offer through [Jesus'] name, and which Jesus the Christ enjoined us to offer, that is, in the Eucharist of the bread and the cup, and which are presented by Christians in all places throughout the world, bears witness that they are well-pleasing to him. But he utterly rejects those presented by you and by those priests of yours, saying, "And I will not accept your sacrifices at your hands; for from the rising of the sun to its setting my name is glorified among the Gentiles (he says), but you profane it."[6]

In other words, the Christian Eucharist is the pure sacrifice foretold by the prophet Malachi. Justin is even more explicit in another part of the *Dialogue*:

> And the offering of fine flour, sirs, which was prescribed to be presented on behalf of those purified from leprosy, was a type of the bread of the Eucha-

---

[5] Oskar Skarsaune, *The Proof from Prophecy: A Study in Justin Martyr's Proof-Text Tradition* (Leiden: E. J. Brill, 1987), 467.

[6] Justin, *Dialogue with Trypho* 117.

rist, the celebration of which our Lord Jesus Christ prescribed, in remembrance of the suffering which he endured on behalf of those who are purified in soul from all iniquity, in order that we may at the same time thank God for having created the world, with all things therein, for the sake of man, and for delivering us from the evil in which we were, and for utterly overthrowing principalities and powers by him who suffered according to his will. Hence God speaks by the mouth of Malachi, one of the twelve [prophets], as I said before, about the sacrifices at that time presented by you: "I have no pleasure in you, says the Lord; and I will not accept your sacrifices at your hands: for, from the rising of the sun unto the going down of the same, my name has been glorified among the Gentiles, and in every place incense is offered to my name, and a pure offering: for my name is great among the Gentiles, says the Lord: but you profane it." He thus speaks of those Gentiles, namely us, who in every place offer sacrifices to him, i.e., the bread of the Eucharist, and also the cup of the Eucharist, affirming both that we glorify his name, and that you profane [it]. The command of circumcision, again, bidding [them] always circumcise the children on the eighth day, was a type of the true circumcision, by which we are circumcised from deceit and iniquity through him who rose from the dead on the first day after the Sabbath, our Lord Jesus Christ.[7]

---

[7] Justin, *Dialogue with Trypho* 41.

To be fair, however, Justin has to admit that his Jewish opponents also interpret Malachi as speaking about prayer as the sacrifice God will accept. In their reading, Malachi was talking about the prayers of Jews scattered throughout the nations—which is still a common Jewish interpretation of Malachi today. According to Justin, what makes that interpretation wrong is that the Jews still aren't everywhere from sunrise to sunset. And Malachi couldn't have been talking about the prayers of the Dispersion in his own time, because the Jews hadn't been dispersed yet.

> But as to you and your teachers deceiving yourselves when you interpret what the Scripture says as referring to those of your nation then in dispersion, and maintain that their prayers and sacrifices offered in every place are pure and well-pleasing, learn that you are speaking falsely, and trying by all means to cheat yourselves: for, first of all, not even now does your nation extend from the rising to the setting of the sun, but there are nations among which none of your race ever dwelt.[8]

These are strong words—but not stronger than you might have in a drawn-out argument with a friend. And then Justin goes back to Malachi to show how well the Christians fulfill his prophecy:

> For there is not one single race of men, whether barbarians, or Greeks, or whatever they may be called,

[8] Justin, *Dialogue with Trypho* 117.

nomads, or vagrants, or herdsmen living in tents, among whom prayers and giving of thanks are not offered through the name of the crucified Jesus. And then, as the Scriptures show, at the time when Malachi wrote this, your dispersion over all the earth, which now exists, had not taken place.[9]

. . . .

Justin ends his dialogue with Trypho and his Jewish friends unconverted, but still friendly. They're happy to have had such a deep discussion of the Scriptures, even if they couldn't come to an agreement. "But since you are on the eve of departure," Trypho tells Justin, "and expect daily to set sail, do not hesitate to remember us as friends when you are gone."

Of course this is Justin making up the story, so he can have his characters do whatever he likes. But it's revealing that he chooses to leave his Jewish friends unconverted but well-disposed. It sounds like a good Christian attitude.

It's especially interesting because Justin might have had good reasons for thinking bad thoughts about Trypho in particular. He makes Trypho a refugee from the late Jewish revolt, and that was a war that had not been pleasant for Christians.

In modern times, we've heard so much—and rightly so—about Christians oppressing Jews that it's hard to remember there was a time when it could be the other way around. Back in the early days of Christianity, though, Christians were far outnumbered by non-Christian Jews in most of the

---

[9] Justin, *Dialogue with Trypho* 117.

known world, but especially in Palestine.

There were two great Jewish revolts about sixty years apart. The first, which began in the 60s (AD), ended in disastrous defeat—but only after the Roman Empire poured all its might into crushing it. In fact, the Judean rebels were embarrassingly successful at first.

The intense wave of nationalism meant that everything that wasn't distinctly Jewish was suspect. There was strong pressure on patriotic Jews not to take up Greek learning, for example. And it was only natural to ask the question: whose side are the Christians on?

After the Jewish War there was one last, desperate attempt to reestablish an independent Jewish state, this one led by Simon Bar Kokhba in the 130s. The stakes were high: failure meant absolute destruction and the death of everyone involved in the revolt. And desperation meant ruthlessness. There could be no neutrality in this conflict—to the rebels, you were with us and drafted, or against us and dead. The Christians were against: Jewish Christians refused to be part of the rebellion, and the rebels took some extreme measures against them.

This is the rebellion from which Trypho is supposed to be a refugee. Thus it certainly reveals something about Justin's character that, when he imagines debating a Jewish rebel who would probably have wanted to kill him not long before, he imagines them ending up as friends.

There's something almost heroically charitable about it, in fact—because the line between Christianity and Judaism was hardening, and it would have been easy to descend into name-calling and abuse. There would be plenty of that to come, though.

We've started with Justin Martyr because he sets the tone for the rest of our story. Everything is already clear and in place with Justin: in particular, the idea of the Eucharist as the pure sacrifice Malachi foretold and the idea of Christians as the new chosen people of God. Salvation has come to the nations, but there has also been a parting of the ways between Judaism and Christianity.

And Christians of the day were certain that Malachi had seen it all centuries before it happened.

CHAPTER 2

MY MESSENGER

WHO WAS THIS MALACHI, ANYWAY?

We really know nothing about him; we may not even know his name. "Malachi" means "my messenger" in Hebrew, which sounds almost like a generic pseudonym for a prophet.

But we do know that he was a prophet in the great tradition of Hebrew prophecy. His job was to tell the people in authority things they might not want to hear. In modern terms, he spoke truth to power. As a famous Bible scholar puts it, "The prophets could always be counted on to strike hard at complacency and triumphalism."[1] And we know that Malachi's big concern was the sacrifices in the Temple.

According to Malachi, the priests weren't taking the sacrifices seriously anymore. Worse, they were showing open contempt for the sacrifices by offering the worst instead of the best. *God*, says Malachi, *doesn't want lousy sacrifices like those. He wishes the Temple would just be shut completely so*

---

[1] Eugene H. Maly, *Prophets of Salvation* (New York: Herder and Herder, 1967), 188.

that those sacrifices wouldn't be offered at all. And then, in his prophetic vision, Malachi sees the perfect sacrifice—a pure sacrifice offered all over the world, in every place and time.

But why is it important that God should get a sacrifice at all? Does God really need sacrifices?

To understand the answer, we have to learn how to think about sacrifices again. The world has almost forgotten what a sacrifice is, and we have to think of it from Malachi's point of view before we can understand his burning indignation against the powerful and lazy priests in Jerusalem.

· · · · · · ·

Imagine yourself getting ready for church. You're putting some care into picking out your best clothes—maybe a formal dress or a suit with matching tie would be a bit old-fashioned, but you still want to look presentable. You're going to God's house, after all.

Now you've arrived, and you're joining the streams of parishioners going in through the big double doors. You have time for a few quick greetings, but as usual you're running a bit later than you'd hoped. The only seats left are up near the front, and by the time you sit down the drone of conversation is already fading. A hush falls as the priest appears in front of the magnificently decorated altar. The sacrifice is about to begin.

Now the attention of the congregation turns to the side door. A man walks in holding the end of a rope, and as he comes further in you can see that on the other end of the rope is an enormous bull. It shambles in behind him, looking confused.

The priest joins the man with the bull and holds it still while the man leans against the animal with both hands—apparently a symbolic gesture of some sort since it doesn't seem to accomplish anything. Then, together, they lead the bull to the altar, where the priest picks up a knife. There's a horrible bellowing roar, mercifully shortened as the priest quickly slits the bull's throat.

Blood gushes everywhere. It pours on the floor around the altar, where it collects in channels that keep it from running out into the congregation. The priest picks up a shallow dish, scoops up some of the blood, and flings it against the altar.

That would probably be the last time you'd ever see the inside of that church. You'd be running for the doors already, in fact, maybe pulling out your phone along the way to call the police.

But for thousands of years of human history, blood was what you saw if you went to worship. Blood was what worship *meant*. If someone from the time of Jacob or Solomon or Moctezuma II saw our liturgy today, it would be baffling. Where is the *sacrifice*? Where is the *blood*?

> Indeed, under the law almost everything is purified
> with blood, and without the shedding of blood there
> is no forgiveness of sins. (Heb 9:22)

Wherever we look in the ancient world, we find bloody sacrifices. In Greece a general wouldn't go into battle without having the entrails of a sacrifice examined for signs that would predict a favorable outcome. On the steppes of central Asia, horses were sacrificed by tribes that depended on the swiftness of the horse for their very existence. In Palestine the Canaanites burned their firstborn children. In Mexico the Aztecs industrialized human sacrifice, fighting endless wars whose main purpose was to capture thousands of sacrificial victims.

Sacrifice is universal. All the religions of the Greek and Roman world did it. The Israelites did it. And *Christianity does it too.* When we understand how Christianity fits—how it fulfills and is the final culmination of that universal drive to sacrifice—then we'll be able to see why the early Christians seem to be obsessed with that one prophecy from Malachi.

· · · · · · ·

The first time the Bible explicitly mentions sacrifice is all the way back in the fourth chapter of Genesis, where Cain and Abel both offer sacrifices to the Lord. Cain's is rejected—the story implies that it's because Cain isn't "doing well": "If you do well, will you not be accepted?" (Gen 4:7). That implies, of course, that Abel *is* doing well, which is why his sacrifice is approved of.

Right in the beginning, then, the principle is established: it's not just what you sacrifice, or how you perform the ritual; the most important thing is what's in the heart of the person making the sacrifice.

Of course we know what was in Cain's heart, because we know what happened next. Cain was so envious of his brother's success that he killed Abel—the first murder recorded in the Bible. But it wouldn't be the last. And murder takes many forms, as the later prophets will point out.

We see sacrifices all through the Old Testament after that. The Law of Moses would establish a whole system of ritual sacrifices for the Israelites. But even before Moses, the Patriarchs never neglected sacrifices. Many of the most memorable stories of Abraham's life, for example, involve sacrifice—especially the most memorable of them all, in which God told Abraham to sacrifice his beloved son, and Abraham was willing to obey.

Abraham also made sacrifices to mark *covenants*—agreements that made a permanent relationship between the parties. The covenant was sealed with the blood of a sacrificial victim. One such covenant was with God himself (see Gen 16:7–21), forming an unbreakable, permanent relationship between God and Abraham. Much later, when the covenant between God and the nation of Israel (Abraham's descendants) was ratified, half of the blood of a victim was sprinkled on the altar and the other half on the people to mark the permanent relationship established between them (see Exod 24:7–8).

All the different kinds of sacrifices have something in common: the idea that we give God what's most valuable to us. Of all things, life is the very most valuable, which is why so many sacrifices are bloody. "For the life of every creature is the blood of it" (Lev 17:14). That's true in a very literal and obvious way: we live only as long as the blood keeps flowing. If the blood drains out, we die. So when we offer blood, we're offering life itself.

Animal blood has life in it, but human blood is far more valuable. The whole idea of human sacrifice is so primally frightful to us today that it's a favorite subject for horror or adventure movies. But there must have been something powerfully attractive about it. The people of Israel, whose religion absolutely prohibited it, were always tempted to imitate the human sacrifices of their Canaanite neighbors—and often enough they just couldn't resist that temptation.

And the attractive thing may have been that human sacrifice just makes sense. Of course if you really want God on your side, you need to give him the most valuable thing you've got, and that would be a human life. What else can you give as a gift to the God who has everything?

So we have to understand that the idea of human sacrifice is, in a very important way, *right,* before we can completely understand the idea of sacrifice.

After all, we can never repay God what we owe him. He created us and the world we live in. Literally every good thing we have is God's doing.

Because the Israelites were so often tempted to go beyond God's instructions in their sacrifices, the Law of Moses was very strict on where and by whom sacrifices could be offered. Priests came from only one of the twelve tribes, the tribe of Levi. And once the people had permanently settled in their new homeland, God would choose a place for his name to dwell, where all sacrifices for him would be offered.

That place, as it turned out, was Jerusalem.

Jerusalem had held out longer than the surrounding area, but David, the ideal king of Israel, conquered it and made it his capital. His son Solomon built a magnificent temple to God there, and that Temple was the only place sacrifices to the God of Israel could legitimately be made. If you were faithful to the Law, you had to bring your sacrifice to Jerusalem no matter how far away you lived, and only the authorized priests could offer it for you.

That system was meant to overcome Israel's problems with imitating the neighbors' religions, but it created problems of its own. Priests had a guaranteed living from the sacrifices, and they soon became corrupt.

At least that's what the prophets said.

. . . .

The priesthood was hereditary, but prophets had a special, individual calling from God. As the biblical scholar Fr. Thomas Lane points out, there could easily have been some bad feelings between the two groups.[2] Doubtless the priests thought some of the prophets were interfering busybodies who had no idea how much work was really involved in being a Temple priest and should mind their own business. The prophets often thought the priests had grown fat and lazy—and their side of the controversy is mostly the one that survives.

Since the priests had positions they hadn't worked for, were supported from the people's tithes and sacrifices no matter how poorly they did their job, and had great influence in Jerusalem, we can easily imagine that the prophets may have had a point. There wasn't much motivation to excel, and the temptation to greed and laziness must have been strong.

Micah says that the priests (and prophets as well) took money for their duties (Mic 3:11). Hosea says that the priests had "forgotten the law of your God" (Hos 4:6) and suggests that the sin offerings, of which the priests received a part, motivated the priests to encourage sin: "They feed on the sin

---

[2] For all these instances of prophets condemning the priesthood, and for the rivalry of priest versus prophet, see Thomas J. Lane, *The Catholic Priesthood: Biblical Foundations* (Steubenville, OH: Emmaus Road, 2016), 18–19.

of my people; they are greedy for their iniquity" (Hos 4:8). Jeremiah, who was a priest himself, says that the Temple had become a "den of robbers" (Jer 7:11)—a condemnation Jesus quoted when he drove out the merchants and money-changers (Matt 21:13).

When we come to Malachi, we find him condemning the priests as the other prophets did. And it's not just that they don't do the sacrifices exactly according to Moses' directions. Malachi is more worried about the state of their hearts:

> Beyond the ritual misdemeanors, it is the fundamental religious attitude that is involved. The involuntary admission that escapes from the priests speaks the truth. God is profaned by this attitude expressing itself in such practices.[3]

To Malachi, the sin of the priests is the sin of Cain. They're not giving God acceptable sacrifices because sin is crouching at their doors. The heart is the problem, not the sacrifice itself.

So there's a long prophetic tradition of condemning the Temple cult, and Malachi falls right into it. If he goes further than any of the others, it's not by a huge leap.

What would have shocked Malachi's original audience most was not that he condemned the priests—prophets were always condemning priests. The shocking thing was that he seemed to condemn the Temple itself.

Sacrifices to Israel's God could only take place in the

[3] Théophane Chary, *Aggée—Zacharie—Malachie* (Paris: J. Gabalda et Cie, 1969), 239, new translation.

Temple. That was central to the whole idea of sacrifice, as far as the Jewish establishment was concerned.[4] So when Malachi told the people that God wanted to see the Temple doors closed and the sacrifices stopped, they probably didn't know quite what to make of that. Was he exaggerating? But then came that other shock: the idea that, somehow, the nations were offering a pure sacrifice when the priests in Jerusalem weren't. What did Malachi mean by that?

Since Malachi speaks in the present tense, he may have meant that the pagans were already offering a purer sacrifice than the Jerusalem priests. Some interpreters have made that argument. Judea was part of the huge Persian Empire, and Zoroastrianism—the favored religion of the Persians—involved bloodless sacrifices. But those certainly weren't universal. "It is unlikely," says the doctrinal historian Edward J. Kilmartin, "that the prophet had in mind a form of worship existing at that time either among the pagans or Jews of the diaspora. The characteristics of this new sacrifice, its purity and universality, make it improbable that he was thinking of any sacrificial practice then in use."[5]

So Malachi didn't mean that the pagans were currently offering that pure sacrifice to God. He was describing a vision of the future.

And if the nations would be sacrificing to God, that meant they would have a change of religion; they would be converted to the worship of Israel's God at some point in

---

[4] Maria-Zoe Petropoulou, *Animal Sacrifice in Ancient Greek Religion, Judaism, and Christianity, 100 BC to AD 200* (Oxford: Oxford University Press, 2008), 118.

[5] Edward J. Kilmartin, SJ, *The Eucharist in the Primitive Church* (Englewood Cliffs, NJ: Prentice-Hall, 1965), 3.

the future.

In Malachi's time, converting the Gentiles certainly wasn't a priority for the remainder of Israel. Their God was the only true God, but they were his chosen people. This stuff about the Gentiles worshiping the God of Israel must have sounded strange, maybe unpatriotic or even seditious.

Yet, Malachi wasn't alone in this prediction. He was the last, and maybe the clearest, of the prophets who made that statement, but he certainly wasn't the only one to announce that salvation would come to all people.

> It shall come to pass in the latter days
>> that the mountain of the house of the LORD
>> shall be established as the highest of the moun-
>>> tains,
>> and shall be raised above the hills;
>> and all the nations shall flow to it,
>> and many peoples shall come, and say:
>> "Come, let us go up to the mountain of the
>>> LORD,
>> to the house of the God of Jacob;
>> that he may teach us his ways
>> and that we may walk in his paths."
>> For out of Zion shall go forth the law,
>> and the word of the LORD from Jerusalem.
>> (Isa 2:2–3)

> The wolf shall dwell with the lamb,
> and the leopard shall lie down with the kid,
> and the calf and the lion and the fatling together,
> and a little child shall lead them. . . .

In that day the root of Jesse shall stand as an
ensign to the peoples; him shall the nations
seek, and his dwellings shall be glorious. (Isa
11:6, 10)

O Lord, my strength and my stronghold,
my refuge in the day of trouble,
to thee shall the nations come
from the ends of the earth and say:
"Our fathers have inherited nought but lies,
worthless things in which there is no profit.
Can man make for himself gods?
Such are no gods!"
(Jer 16:19–20)

Many peoples and strong nations shall come to
seek the Lord of hosts in Jerusalem, and to
entreat the favor of the Lord. (Zech 8:22)

The same is true of Malachi's strong denunciation of the
current priesthood. Other prophets were equally clear that
the priesthood was corrupt and about to be swept away:

An appalling and horrible thing
has happened in the land:
the prophets prophesy falsely,
and the priests rule at their direction;

my people love to have it so,
but what will you do when the end comes?
(Jer 5:30–31)

The early Christians saw themselves as heirs of that same prophetic tradition. When they condemned the Jewish establishment, they spoke with Jeremiah, Hosea, Micah, Hosea, Zephaniah, and Malachi, who had all condemned the same establishment—and condemned it vigorously. When they announced that salvation had come to the whole world, not just Israel, they were announcing the fulfillment of the prophecies everyone had heard.

And when the Christians looked at Malachi's prophecy of the worldwide pure offering, they saw the Eucharist. They saw themselves living in the age Malachi foretold.

That identification goes right back to the beginning. All the ancient commentators take it for granted that Jesus is referring directly to Malachi 1:11 with the Samaritan woman at the well:

> The woman said to him, "Sir, I perceive that you are a prophet. Our fathers worshiped on this mountain; and you say that in Jerusalem is the place where men ought to worship." Jesus said to her, "Woman, believe me, the hour is coming when neither on this mountain nor in Jerusalem will you worship the Father. You worship what you do not know; we worship what we know, for salvation is from the Jews. But the hour is coming, and now is, when the true worshipers will worship the Father in spirit and truth, for

such the Father seeks to worship him. God is spirit, and those who worship him must worship in spirit and truth." The woman said to him, "I know that Messiah is coming (he who is called Christ); when he comes, he will show us all things." Jesus said to her, "I who speak to you am he." (John 4:19–26)

Mount Gerizim was (and still is) the holy place of the Samaritans, who reject everything in our Old Testament after the Torah, the five books of Moses (Genesis through Deuteronomy). The woman may genuinely be curious, not sure about what to believe. Or she might be thinking that she can trap Jesus into saying something that will either embarrass him or allow her to reject him and go on comfortably with her ordinary beliefs. But he tells her that the world of Malachi's prophecy is coming—in fact, it's already here, right in front of you. The question of Jerusalem or Mt. Gerizim will be irrelevant, because we're in the world of the pure offering now.

Paul never quotes our verse of Malachi directly. Yet he seems to have it in mind all through his first letter to the Corinthians, his most intensely Eucharistic letter:

Do you not know that you are God's temple and that God's Spirit dwells in you? If any one destroys God's temple, God will destroy him. For God's temple is holy, and that temple you are. (1 Cor 3:16–17)

There's still a Temple, Paul says—still a place for God's name to dwell. But now that place is wherever there's a faithful Christian.

What worries Paul most about the church in Corinth is the disunity he hears about. It's when he talks about the disunity that he brings up his famous institution narrative—an account of the Last Supper probably older than any of the Gospels:

> For, in the first place, when you assemble as a church, I hear that there are divisions among you; and I partly believe it, for there must be factions among you in order that those who are genuine among you may be recognized. When you meet together, it is not the Lord's supper that you eat. For in eating, each one goes ahead with his own meal, and one is hungry and another is drunk. What! Do you not have houses to eat and drink in? Or do you despise the church of God and humiliate those who have nothing? What shall I say to you? Shall I commend you in this? No, I will not.
>
> For I received from the Lord what I also delivered to you, that the Lord Jesus on the night when he was betrayed took bread . . . (1 Cor 11:18–23)

The sign of the true Church is its unity and its universality—its catholicity. Christ is not divided. So if you're all doing your own thing, that's not the Lord's Supper. The true sacrifice is offered as one from the rising of the sun to its setting.

But what were those first Christians really doing when they offered that sacrifice? Was it anything like our worship today? Wouldn't it be wonderful if we had something that would give us a glimpse of that early Christian Church in the time of Paul?

Well, we're very lucky. We do have a glimpse of the early Church—although it nearly got away from us.

CHAPTER 3

THIS IS THAT SACRIFICE

IN 1873 A SINGLE PRECIOUS MANUSCRIPT turned up that set the world of patristic scholarship buzzing. It's a pretty quiet world most of the time, at least to outside observers. But once in a while there's a sensational new discovery that goes off like a bomb.

The explosion in 1873 was caused by a collection of early Christian writings that had been copied from much older manuscripts in the year 1056 and had just been unearthed by an Orthodox metropolitan of Nicomedia, Philotheos Bryennios. Among its treasures was a document headed "Teaching of the Twelve Apostles," followed by the fuller title "Teaching of the Lord Through the Twelve Apostles to the Gentiles." Since then it's been known by the first word of its title in Greek, *Didache* (pronounced *DID-ah-kay*).

Bits and pieces of the *Didache* were known from quoted scraps in other sources, and it had once been a very popular book among the early Christians. In fact, some early churches counted it as canonical Scripture. But as it fell out of use, Christians stopped copying it, and resembling 90% of the literature from ancient times, it disappeared.

Now here it was. And immediately, scholars started arguing, because that's what scholars do.

There were all sorts of arguments to be argued. First of all, when was the *Didache* written? Some scholars insisted that it was one of the earliest extant Christian documents. Others held out for a date as late as the 200s (which would still make it an early Christian document, but not nearly as precious in the eyes of the scholarly world).

Then there was the question of how the *Didache* was related to the books of the New Testament, which of course depended on the date. There are parts of the *Didache* that are very similar to parts of Matthew's Gospel, for example. Were they taken from Matthew? Or did Matthew take those parts of his Gospel from the *Didache?* Or did they both draw on the same oral tradition, or on earlier written documents?

After more than a century of scholarly pushing and pulling, the arguments are far from settled. However, a fairly broad scholarly consensus holds that the *Didache* evolved over time. It's a composite, with some parts of it older than other parts. And the most reputable scholars seem to be settling on an agreement that the oldest parts probably date from before the year 50, which would make them older than the Gospels and contemporary with the earliest letters of Paul. The final form of the document is most likely from about fifty years later, which is still very early.

What makes the question so fascinating is that the *Didache* gives us a vivid picture of the early Church—and if modern scholarship is to be believed, it's a picture of the Church at a time when the apostles were still alive, written down before our New Testament had taken shape.

The most surprising thing about it is that there are no surprises. It shows us a Church we instantly recognize. We see our own liturgy, our own doctrine, our own church organization. They're all in a more primitive state, of course, but already the elements we recognize are there. It looks like the Catholic Church to us.

But to someone who lived in that first century, the Catholic Church would have looked remarkably Jewish.

. . . .

The *Didache* as we have it (in its final form) is a complete instruction manual for setting up a new Christian congregation. From various sources it collects all the information you'll need in one handy document:

- A summary of Christian doctrine to get new converts started.
- Instructions for Baptism (by immersion or sprinkling) and daily prayers and practice.
- A liturgy for the Eucharist.
- Instructions for dealing with traveling representatives of the larger Catholic Church—teachers and prophets.
- Instructions for staffing your local church administration with bishops and deacons.
- And, finally, a brief explanation of what Christians can expect in the end times.

This long-lost book contains everything you need to set up your home-church and make sure it meets the standards of the universal Church. It seems to have been widely used:

fragments of translations into all the common languages of the Mediterranean world have come down to us.

And much of the material either comes from Jewish sources directly or is inspired by Jewish practice. Christians weren't thinking of themselves as practitioners of a new religion. They thought of themselves as true descendants of Abraham and Moses and the prophets, but descendants who were living under new conditions. The Messiah had come, and the world had changed.

Jewish Roots

The *Didache* starts with a summary of Christian doctrine, introduced by a sermon on the Two Ways: "Two ways there are, one of life and one of death, and great is the difference between the two ways."[1]

This sermon would probably have been familiar to any Jewish listener. There's a similar Two Ways discourse in the Dead Sea Scrolls, for example. In the *Didache,* the Two Ways section leads into some of Jesus' teachings that we remember from the Sermon on the Mount. But nothing in those teachings would have struck a Jewish hearer as the least bit unorthodox. The Christians would seem to be a Jewish group repeating the teachings of their favorite rabbi.[2]

When the *Didache* speaks of the Eucharist, we recognize something very much like our modern Christian liturgy. However, scholars identify the Eucharistic prayers as vari-

[1] *Didache* 1:1.
[2] Everett Ferguson, "Didache," in *Encyclopedia of Early Christianity*, ed. Everett Ferguson (New York: Garland, 1990), 262.

ations of familiar Jewish mealtime prayers. The most distinctively Christian ritual, the Eucharist, is accompanied by prayers that are instantly recognizable as Jewish.

And why are these people celebrating the Eucharist? Because this is that age Malachi saw long ago in his prophetic vision.

> And gathering together on the Lord's day of the Lord, break a loaf and give thanks, first confessing your transgressions, so that your sacrifice may be a pure one. But let no one who has something against his companion come together with you while they have not been reconciled, so that your sacrifice may not be polluted. For this is that sacrifice which the Lord proclaimed: "In every place and time offer me a pure sacrifice; because a great King am I, says the Lord, and my name is wonderful among the nations."[3]

So it makes sense that the Eucharistic prayers are Jewish. These are the prayers we've always prayed—fulfilled. "The *Didache*," says one modern scholar, "presents a church still in close proximity to Judaism and still developing its distinctive traditions."[4]

Here, at the very beginning of Christianity, it's already assumed that the Eucharist is a sacrifice. That's not a late theological development; it's central to the Christian understanding of our faith. And it's the very sacrifice Malachi had

---

[3] *Didache* 14.
[4] Ferguson, "Didache," 262.

in mind, the one offered from the rising of the sun to its setting—a phrase that, as one biblical scholar put it, "means the whole world and an unlimited measure of time,"[5] as the *Didache* interprets it as well. Scripture was usually quoted from memory—poor people, as most of the earliest Christians were, didn't have books lying around—so the wording may not be exact. Nevertheless, the quotation from Malachi is unmistakable. The *Didache* is a handy manual of what it means to be a Christian, and to be a Christian is to realize that we're living in the age Malachi foresaw.

"The Lord's Day of the Lord," incidentally, is an obviously redundant expression. A few interpreters see it as referring to a Christian celebration of Yom Kippur, the Jewish Day of Atonement. But what we see in the *Didache* is our regular Sunday liturgy, and in every other early Christian writing, the "Lord's day" is Sunday. That doesn't mean, however, that there's no connection to Yom Kippur. The Day of Atonement, like the Passover and every other feast of the Law of Moses, is taken up in the Eucharist, so Sunday takes over for Yom Kippur, as the Jewish commentator Daniel Stökel ben Ezra points out.[6] Christians don't reject the sacrificial cult of the Old Testament; they believe that the sacrifice of Jesus Christ fulfilled all the sacrifices and the feasts in the Law of Moses. And the Eucharist is that sacrifice, offered throughout time and space.

Furthermore, it's not only Christians who see the sacri-

---

[5] P. Bonaventura Mariani, OFM, "De Sacrificio a Malachia praedicto," in *Antonianum* 9 (Rome: Pontificia Università Antonianum, 1934), 362.

[6] Daniel Stökl Ben Ezra, *The Impact of Yom Kippur on Early Christianity* (Tubingen: Mohr Siebeck, 2003), 217.

ficial nature of the Mass. From the Jewish point of view, the similarity between the Mass and the old Temple cult is clear:

> "Christianity adopted the policy of sanctifying space, as Judaism had once done. Christian worship in the form of the traditional mass affords the devout an experience of sacrifice, of communion, and proclaims that God is present. The Christian church, then, is a temple."[7]

These words are from The Jewish Publication Society's Torah Commentary series, the volume on Leviticus, in an essay called "Leviticus in the Ongoing Jewish Tradition." The author contrasts Catholicism with Islam, which is actually more like modern Judaism in its "nonsacral worship." For this one Jewish commentator, the thing that makes Christianity strikingly *different* from today's Judaism is that Christianity seems to have retained *more* of the Temple tradition of ancient Israel.

But in the time when the earliest parts of the *Didache* were written, that distinction wouldn't have been obvious. The Temple sacrifices were still going on in Jerusalem, and the Temple was still the focus of Jewish worship. Christians worshiped there too, as we see in the Acts of the Apostles (see, for example, Acts 2:46 and 5:42). Sometimes Christians were thrown out of synagogues after heated arguments. But the fact that they were thrown out means that they were in

---

[7] Baruch A. Levine, "Leviticus in the Ongoing Jewish Tradition," in *Leviticus*, The JPS Torah Commentary (Philadelphia: Jewish Publication Society, 1989), 216.

there. They didn't see themselves as something separate from
the ancient tradition of Israel. They saw themselves as Jews
who had gotten it right.[8]

In fact, the Christian movement was one of many different groups in Judaism, some others of which—like the
people who gave us the Dead Sea Scrolls—had also separated themselves from the Temple cult in Jerusalem, and
would probably have gotten themselves thrown out of a lot
of synagogues. There wasn't just one kind of Judaism: it was
a rainbow of different sects and styles of thinking. Back then
it would have been easy to see the Christian movement as
just one more of those different sects.

Just a few years later, though, things would change radically.

. . . .

Two big things accelerated the separation of Christians
from Jews. One was the great fire in Rome in the year 64,
and the other was the Jewish revolt that began simmering at
about the same time.

The great fire devastated the city of Rome, and rumors
blamed the emperor Nero for it. Nero was at least erratic if
not mad, and his history of extravagant behavior made the
rumors plausible. Why had he set it? Because he wanted to
clear a space for his palace, said one rumor. (In fact, Nero did
almost immediately start building an immense palace that
covered a huge part of the burned-out area.) Because he just

8 For an interesting discussion of the dispute over Temple piety, see
Matthew J. Thomas, *Paul's 'Works of the Law' in the Perspective of Second
Century Reception* (Tubingen: Mohr Siebeck, 2018), 65–66.

50

wanted to enjoy the spectacle, said another rumor. They said he watched the flames from a distance and sang a song he'd made up about the burning of Troy.

Whether the rumors were true or not, they were bad publicity. Nero needed someone to blame. And the Christians were perfect for the part. The Roman historian Tacitus, who obviously had contempt for Christians, is nevertheless very clear that they suffered only because Nero needed an underdog to condemn:

> So, to squash the rumor, Nero attached the guilt to, and inflicted the most dreadful penalties on, certain persons infamous for their abominations, whom the people called Christians. The originator of their name, Christ, had been executed in the reign of Tiberius, under the procurator Pontius Pilate. The pernicious superstition, repressed for a moment, erupted again, not only throughout Judea, but even in the city [Rome], where all the dreadful or shameful things in the world come together and become all the rage. Therefore at first those who confessed were arrested, and then, on their information, an enormous multitude was convicted not so much of the crime of arson as of hatred of the human species.[9]

Now that he had his scapegoats, Nero exercised his usual creativity in making a public spectacle out of them. He invited all of Rome to a lavish after-dark garden party, in which Christians were made into cheerful torches to light up the

---

[9]   Tacitus, *Annals* 15.44.

night, and came up with all kinds of clever tortures to entertain the sadistic Roman public. But Tacitus thought that even the citizens were not quite heartless enough for Nero's severity: no matter how deserving the Christians were of the worst punishments, people could see that they were suffering not because it was necessary to the public, but just to satisfy Nero's own cruelty. They began to pity the Christians, which in Tacitus' opinion was the worst result that could have come about.

Tacitus was a little boy when the great fire happened, so we should take his word for it that he did his research. It's possible that he attributes his own later opinion of Christians to the Romans of Nero's time.

But Nero's choice of the Christians as scapegoats suggests two things: there were enough of them that people were getting worried about them, and they were beginning to be distinguishable from regular Jews. Tradition says that Peter and Paul both died in this flurry of violence under Nero, which supports that in some way they had made themselves visible as leaders of the sect.

At any rate, Nero's persecution certainly would have encouraged other Jews to make a sharp distinction between themselves and Christians. If you didn't want to end up as a torch at the emperor's garden party, you probably took care to explain why you weren't one of *them*. There were probably tens of thousands of Jews in Rome at the time, and at most a few thousand Christians. Nero's empress Poppaea was at least very sympathetic to the Jews, if not a Jewish convert, so she may well have taught Nero to make that vital distinction between Jews and Christians.

After the fire, things settled down. But in the Roman

government the distinction had been made, and the principle had been established. Now the Christians were a known illegal sect, and they could be arrested any time some government official was feeling ambitious, or any time some neighbor with a grudge felt like reporting them.

Meanwhile, over on the other side of the world, the Jews of Palestine were getting more and more restless as the Roman administration seemed to be getting more and more tone-deaf. Just two years after the Roman fire, the tension in the East erupted into open rebellion when the Roman authorities plundered the Temple to get the money the locals were refusing to hand over in taxes.

The Christians, according to Christian historians, left Jerusalem as soon as the trouble started. They remembered Jesus' warning: "then let those who are in Judea flee to the mountains; let him who is on the housetop not go down to take what is in his house; and let him who is in the field not turn back to take his mantle" (Matt 24:16–18). So they headed for the hills, just as he had told them to do.

It was amazing, and frightening to the Romans, how successful the rebels were at first. But not everyone was in sympathy with the revolt, and when the Romans brought in their two most talented generals—Vespasian and his son Titus, both of whom would later be emperors—things started to go badly for the revolutionaries. When Galilee was lost, Jerusalem filled up with refugees, and civil war started between different factions there. At last the Romans took the city, and in the year 70, they destroyed the Temple. Jesus' prophecy had come to pass: "Truly, I say to you, there will not be left here one stone upon another, that will not be thrown down" (Matt 24:2).

That was the end of the Temple sacrifices. The center of all Jewish worship was gone; the entire focus of the religion had to be reimagined.

What came out of their new vision was something much more like the Judaism we know today. The prayers of the faithful would be the only sacrifices they could offer—although the faithful continued to pray that the sacrifices would be restored in Jerusalem one day. And as Christians became more common, the Jews who were not Christian began to define themselves more and more as "not-Christian." They emphasized the differences: their own fidelity to the Law of Moses became much more important in their self-identification.

The distinction for them was important because Christians were popping up everywhere, continuing to claim they were the true descendants of Israel. And they were telling people that the Law of Moses had been fulfilled in one perfect sacrifice—the one foreseen centuries ago by the prophet Malachi.

. . . .

Already, even a few years after the birth of the Church, there were Christian sleeper cells popping up all over the known world. From the very beginning of Christianity, Christians believed that their duty was to spread the Good News throughout the world. "Go therefore and make disciples of all nations," Jesus told his apostles, "baptizing them in the name of the Father and of the Son and of the Holy Spirit" (Matt 28:19). We call it the Great Commission—the very last instruction Jesus gives in the Gospel of Matthew.

According to tradition, the apostles divided up the world and went in all directions—Thomas as far as India; James (in one tradition) all the way to Spain. We know that Paul had also at least planned to visit Spain (see Rom 15:24). Historians are divided on whether he ever got there, but the point is that he took his mission seriously. He was going to spread the Gospel literally to the ends of the earth: Spain was the westernmost point not just of the Roman Empire but of the known world as well.

But even as active as the apostles were, the Good News traveled faster than any of them could carry it. The Roman Empire covered the world from Britain to Arabia, and its trade reached over to China and deep into Africa. New converts traveled hither and yon in the thousands of ships that plied the seas, or along the thousands of miles of paved Roman superhighways. Everywhere they went, they couldn't help sharing the Good News. Others who heard it would be intrigued, and another local church would start.

Thus the *Didache*. Something like it was needed, something to set the local church going until an official representative of the universal Church could arrive. Of all its various instructions, not the least important are the ones about receiving traveling apostles and prophets, including some advice about how to tell the true ones from the false ones. (If they stayed more than two days, they were false ones. That gives us a vivid picture of how busy the true apostles must have been visiting all these Christian congregations popping up everywhere.)

So Christians were all over the Roman Empire and the world outside it as well, penetrating into every town and village, "like leaven which a woman took and hid in three measures of meal, till it was all leavened" (Matt 13:33).

Eventually the Roman Empire was bound to notice. And the struggle that followed would amplify the sacrificial emphasis of Christianity—even as it drove Christianity and post-Temple Judaism further apart.

CHAPTER 4

IGNATIUS OF ANTIOCH
BECOMES THE EUCHARIST

A LITTLE AFTER THE YEAR 100, the bishop of Antioch, a man named Ignatius, was arrested and sent to Rome for the final execution of his sentence. Presumably he would be given one last chance to recant his Christianity and make a token sacrifice to the genius of the emperor to prove he had gotten over his ridiculous delusion. The Romans were very generous that way: they could think of all sorts of ingenious tortures for Christians, but they made the tortures very easy to avoid. At any point in the process, you could just walk away free. All you had to do was curse Christ and make the proper pagan sacrifice.

We know about Ignatius because on his way from Antioch in Syria (at the far eastern edge of the Empire) to the capital of Rome in the west, he wrote seven letters—at least seven that have survived and are generally agreed upon to be the authentic work of Ignatius. Together they tell the story of a man on his way to martyrdom who wonders whether he'll really be worthy to earn that crown. But he hopes he will so that he can become part of the pure offering Malachi foresaw. He has begun to see everything in terms of the Eucharist—especially his own impending martyrdom.

· · · · · · ·

We don't actually know much about Ignatius other than what he tells us about himself. But here's what we do know: Ignatius was bishop of Antioch in Syria (though it's now in the far southeast of Turkey) for some time before he was arrested in the early 100s. The reason for his arrest isn't exactly stated, but in his letters it's implied that it had something to do with his Christianity. This was during the reign of the emperor Trajan, who famously formulated a "don't ask, don't tell" policy for the Christians: provincial governors were not to go hunting for Christians, who were to be arrested only on reliable information—and the informer had better be right, because if he was found to be lying, he would suffer the penalty his victim would have suffered. Christians generally remembered Trajan fondly because of this policy, which allowed most of them to live out their lives in peace. But bishops were often targets too big to ignore.

The crime must have been considered an important one, because Ignatius was packed off to Rome under the guard of "ten leopards—that is, a detachment of soldiers—who, when they are well treated, become even worse."[1] Maybe by making a very public spectacle of one of the Christians' most prominent leaders, the authorities hoped they would break up the sect. Whatever the reason, Ignatius was on his way to Rome, where he knew he would die—if everything went correctly.

[1] Ignatius, *Epistle to the Romans* 5.1.

Along the way he planned to stop and visit a number of prominent churches, but a last-minute change of route forced him to rely on letters to several of them instead, which would be conveyed by representatives who came out from those churches to meet him. That's very fortunate for us, because those letters give us our most vivid picture of the Christian Church just after the year 100. And, of course, they also give us a realistic look at one of the Church's most colorful characters.

Ignatius was determined to die a martyr. He hadn't gone looking for this martyrdom, but now that it had come his way he wasn't going to miss it. "No point for me in the ends of the world, or the kingdoms of this age. Better for me to die for Jesus Christ than to be a king over the ends of the earth. I seek the one who died for us; I long for the one who rose again for us. The birth-pangs have come over me."[2]

· · · · · · ·

Ignatius's city, Antioch, was the place where the name "Christian" had first been used for followers of Jesus Christ (see Acts 11:26)—quite possibly as a derogatory term at first. It was a city with all the modern conveniences, including a famous system of street lighting that was the envy of other cities, although they apparently didn't envy it enough to spend the money on imitating it. In the time of Ignatius, it was one of the three most important cities in the Roman Empire, after Rome itself and Alexandria in Egypt. Also, Peter had been the head of the church in Antioch before he went to Rome.

---

[2] Ignatius, *Epistle to the Romans* 6.1.

For all these reasons—the significance of the place in general and its significance in the history of the young Church in particular—the bishop of Antioch was one of the most important Christian leaders. The Roman authorities must have thought they had caught a big fish.

Nevertheless, there were more important things than catching Christians. There were bribes, for example. If you gave the Roman authorities a good reason for looking the other way, Ignatius might walk free.

When Ignatius was arrested, his friends from all over the Christian world got to work to try to find some way he could be spared. It was often possible to grease the wheels of justice so that they turned in your favor. You just had to have the right contacts and know what kind of grease they liked.

But Ignatius would have none of that. "I fear that your love might do me an injustice," he wrote to the Christians in Rome. "For it is easy to do what you wish to do, but difficult for me to get to God if you don't spare me."[3] He would never have an opportunity like this again, Ignatius said. "Have patience with me: what suits me I myself know."[4]

He understood that his friends wanted what they thought was best for him, but they had to understand that he really was hoping for the Romans to kill him. "I write to you alive, but in love with death."[5]

The Greeks distinguished different kinds of love: there was brotherly love, and the selfless love of one Christian for another. But there was also passionate love, the love of a man

---

[3] Ignatius, *Epistle to the Romans* 1.2.

[4] Ignatius, *Epistle to the Romans* 5.3.

[5] Ignatius, *Epistle to the Romans* 7.2.

for a beautiful woman, and that's the kind of love Ignatius uses when he says he's in love with death. He doesn't mean he thinks it's a good idea; he means he loves death like a mistress.

But why is Ignatius so bent on dying? He explains to the Christians in Smyrna that it's because Jesus really did suffer for him.

There were already people who denied the reality of Jesus' death. Perhaps out of excessive love for Jesus, or at least wrongly placed love, they couldn't bring themselves to believe that all those terrible things had really happened to the Son of God. So they imagined that he had only *seemed* to die on the cross—a heresy known as "Docetism," from the Greek word for "seeming."

But if that was the case, then there's nothing worthwhile about sharing Jesus' pain, because Jesus didn't really suffer. Ignatius tells the Smyrnaeans that his whole journey toward martyrdom is a repudiation of that kind of Docetism:

> For if our Lord *seemed* to be doing these things, then
> I *seem* to have been put in chains. And also, why have
> I handed myself over to death by fire, by dagger, or
> by beasts? But near to the dagger, near to God; in
> among the beasts, in there with God—only in the
> name of Jesus Christ, for the purpose of suffering
> with him. I am patient with it all, since he, the per-
> fect man, gives me the power.[6]

Our suffering is worth something because the suffering of Jesus was real. He really made that sacrifice, and we can

---

[6] Ignatius, *Epistle to the Smyrnaeans* 4.2.

participate in it. All our sufferings are bound up with his in the sacrifice of the Eucharist. In fact, Ignatius expects that, in being consumed by beasts in the arena, he will *become* the Eucharist. To the Romans especially—the Romans who might have the power to have his sentence commuted—he makes the connection explicit:

> I beg you, do not be kind to me at the wrong time. Let me be food for beasts, through which I will be able to reach God. I am the wheat of God, and by the teeth of the beasts let me be ground, so that I may be found pure bread. Rather coax the beasts, so that they may become my tomb and leave nothing of my body, so that when I have passed I may not be any trouble to anyone. Then, truly, I will be a disciple of Jesus Christ, when the world no longer sees my body. Pray to the Lord for me, so that by these means I may prove a sacrifice to God.[7]

Ignatius tells the Christians in Ephesus that they should pray for all their persecutors, "for there is in them the hope of repentance, so that they may find God."[8]

> Let us be seen as their brothers by our mildness; let us work hard to be imitators of the Lord in who shall be more wronged, robbed, or ignored, so that the devil may not go grazing among you.[9]

---

[7] Ignatius, *Epistle to the Romans* 4.
[8] Ignatius, *Epistle to the Ephesians* 10.
[9] Ignatius, *Epistle to the Smyrnaeans* 10.1, 3.

When we do these things, we're not just being careful about our own salvation. We're joining in a cosmic act of love; we're *living* that perfect sacrifice Malachi foresaw.

> More than this do not grant me: to be poured out as a libation to God while yet an altar stands ready, so that, forming a chorus in love, you may sing to the Father in Jesus Christ, because God has found the bishop of Syria worthy to be found at the setting of the sun, having summoned him from its rising.[10]

This entire journey is a fulfillment of Malachi's prophecy. Joining his suffering to Christ's, Ignatius is swept up in Malachi's ecstatic vision. Moving from the rising of the sun to its setting, Ignatius *becomes* that pure offering. He imagines himself at the center of a sacrificial liturgy, with the Roman Christians singing a glorious hymn to the Father as Ignatius himself becomes the sacrificial offering on God's holy altar.

We can see now why the martyrs could be so enthusiastic. They could see Christ right in front of them on the table of the Eucharist, and they could see Christ in the bodies of their fellow Christians suffering for their faith. None of this sacrificial language was an abstract idea to them. It was a concrete reality they lived every day.

For just that reason it was important to keep their enthusiasm under control. Ignatius himself worried that he might "perish in boasting"; his enthusiasm for martyrdom might run away with him. He constantly asked himself whether he

---

[10] Ignatius, *Epistle to the Romans* 2.2.

was really worthy of standing in for Christ.

> For I would love to suffer, but I don't know if I'm worthy. Because I don't let many people see my eagerness, it assaults me all the more. I therefore crave meekness, by which the ruler of this age is put down.[11]

Meanwhile, though, Ignatius is also worried about the people he's going to leave behind.

· · · · · · ·

Unity is the thing Ignatius most desired for all the churches—and the thing that seems to be most in danger.

> Take care, then, to make use of one Eucharist—for there is one flesh of our Lord Jesus Christ, and one cup unto unity in his blood; one altar, as one bishop, together with the priesthood and the deacons, my fellow servants—so that what you do you do according to God.[12]

That was what Ignatius wrote to the people of Philadelphia, in what is now western Turkey. He was warning them against divisions in the Church, just as Paul had warned his readers earlier (see, for example, 1 Cor 3). The Church is one because the Eucharist is one.

---

[11] Ignatius, *Epistle to the Trallians* 4.2.
[12] Ignatius, *Epistle to the Philadelphians* 4.

Notice, by the way, the description of the three levels of Church hierarchy. You have one bishop in each local church, a group of priests or elders ("presbyters" in Greek), and the deacons. This is exactly what our Catholic Church looks like today, and Ignatius is the first to spell out the organization in this way. Some scholars have tried to argue that Ignatius was the inventor of this one-bishop organization of local churches. But he's writing to people in Philadelphia, not his own diocese of Antioch. And he has already met the representatives of the Philadelphian church: they're the ones who would be carrying back his letter. It wouldn't make any sense to them unless their church was already organized the way he describes it.[13]

Before this, Ignatius knew about divisions in the Church. As bishop in Antioch, he'd had to deal with dissension and difficulties in his own church. Jewish and Gentile Christians worshiped in the same community, but they didn't always like each other. There was probably disharmony of other sorts in this church as well. We don't know exactly what was going on, because we only have Ignatius' letters and he doesn't go into detail.[14]

"Is Christ divided?" Paul had asked rhetorically (1 Cor 1:13). The answer, of course, is no. There is one Christ, and there is one Eucharist. And the Eucharist is the central fact of the Christian religion.

---

[13] Thomas A. Robinson, *Ignatius of Antioch and the Parting of the Ways* (Peabody, MA: Hendrickson, 2009), 100.
[14] Robinson, *Ignatius of Antioch*, 165–166.

Let no one be led astray. Even the heavenly beings, and the glory of the angels, and the rulers both visible and invisible, if they do not believe in the blood of Christ—yes, even they are judged.[15]

The infallible mark of a heretic was not participating in the Eucharistic sacrifice with the rest of the Church:

From the Eucharist and prayer they keep away, since they will not acknowledge the Eucharist to be the flesh of our Savior Jesus Christ.[16]

When salvation came to the whole world, as Malachi had foreseen, it came in the form of that one pure sacrifice. That's why, for Ignatius, unity is the sign of the real Catholic Church, and preserving it is worth a lot of trouble. To his fellow bishop Polycarp, Ignatius wrote, "Keep unity in mind, than which nothing is better."[17] The perfect sacrifice is worldwide and everywhere the same. As Ignatius wrote to the church in Smyrna (now the city of Izmir in western Turkey):

Flee divisions as the origin of evils. All of you, follow the bishop, as Jesus Christ does the Father, and the priesthood as if they were the apostles. And respect the deacons as instituted by God. Without the bishop, let no one do anything concerning the

---

[15] Ignatius, *Epistle to the Smyrnaeans* 6.1.

[16] Ignatius, *Epistle to the Smyrnaeans* 6.2.

[17] Ignatius, *Epistle to Polycarp* 1.2.

church. The Eucharist is valid only if it is under the bishop, or under someone to whom he has entrusted it. Wherever the bishop appears, there let the multitude be; just as, wherever Jesus Christ is, there is the Catholic Church. It is not permitted without the bishop either to baptize or to have an agape [love feast]; but whatever he approves of, that is also pleasing to God, so that everything you do may be both secure and valid.[18]

This is actually the first time we know of that anyone has used the term "Catholic Church" (in Greek, *katholike ekklesia*) in writing to describe the Christian Church. But "Catholic" just means "universal," and the fact that Ignatius uses it in a letter to the church in Smyrna strongly suggests that he didn't invent the term. He expected the Smyrnaeans to understand what he meant. There is one Church, and we all belong to it, or we're not really Christians.

For I have seen you perfected in an immovable faith, just as if you were nailed to the cross of the Lord Jesus Christ both in flesh and in spirit, and anchored in love in the blood of Christ, completely convinced on the subject of our Lord that he is truly from the line of David according to the flesh, Son of God according to the will and power, truly born from a virgin, baptized by John so that all righteousness might be fulfilled by him, truly, under Pontius Pilate and Herod the Tetrarch, nailed for us in the flesh—and

---

[18] Ignatius, *Epistle to the Smyrnaeans* 8.

we are from the fruit of it by his divinely blessed suffering—so that he might raise a flag for all ages through the resurrection for his saints and holy ones, whether among the Jews or among the Gentiles, in the one body of his Church.[19]

This is in effect Ignatius' creed of "catholicity," as he expresses it to the Smyrnaeans. He tells them that he knows they believe it, but he wouldn't be so specific unless he thought it was very important that they should *continue* to believe it. Jew or Gentile, the whole world can be saved by rallying to the flag of Jesus' resurrection in the one *united* Church.

The sign of that unity is the Eucharist, as authorized by the bishop. There is one sacrifice all over the world, from the rising of the sun to its setting. That is what tells us that we're living in Malachi's vision.

But it's also what separates us from the people who still haven't accepted Christ. Or, rather, in Ignatius' way of seeing things, it's what makes them separate themselves. On the one hand, Ignatius shows us a Christian Church that's already very distinct from the Jewish establishment. On the other hand, what makes it distinct is its claim to be more Jewish than the Jews. For Ignatius the Christian Church is the only place where the real sacrifice is offered to the God of Abraham, Moses, and David.

So we're seeing the parting of the ways already in progress: Christianity has already separated, to a large extent, from Judaism and is becoming a recognizably different

[19] Ignatius, *Epistle to the Smyrnaeans* 1.

thing. But the bitter family argument is still just beginning. Each side is claiming to be the true heir of Moses and the prophets, and the argument is only going to get louder.

CHAPTER 5

The Apostolic Fathers
and the True Temple

IGNATIUS IS ONE OF THE PEOPLE we call an "Apostolic Father"—a Christian writer who had known the apostles and picked up where they left off. We have more of Ignatius' writings than we have of most of the rest of the group, but—considering how small the Church was in those days—a surprising number of other Apostolic Fathers have also left us their thoughts.

Along his way to martyrdom, Ignatius wrote one letter to an individual rather than a whole congregation: Polycarp, his fellow bishop, who was head of the church in Smyrna. Later, Polycarp—who tradition says had been made bishop by the apostle John himself—also was martyred after a long and useful life. Once again he was given every opportunity to recant. At one point the proconsul demanded that he join in the crowd's cries of "Away with the atheists!" (Christians were often called atheists because they didn't believe in the pagan gods.) Polycarp cheerfully complied: he turned and held out his arm to indicate the jeering crowd, and said, "Away with the atheists!"

Even after that demonstration, the proconsul still tried to persuade the old man to swear the oath and offer the incense. "What harm is there in it?" the proconsul kept asking. But Polycarp refused. He had been put in a spot where he had to take a stand: deny Christ or die. So he died.

He was sentenced to be burned on a pyre, "like a ram chosen from a great flock for sacrifice," as his followers remembered it, "a burnt offering prepared and acceptable to God."[1] So Ignatius' language about sacrifice is not unique. This was how Christians saw martyrdom. The imagery is from the sacrificial cult of the Temple, but now there is only one sacrifice—Christ's eternal self-offering, with the martyr's suffering joined to it and turned to joy.

Christianity is a sacrificial cult. The big difference from all other sacrificial cults is that our God has made the sacrifice for us. That was the only way Malachi's prophecy could be fulfilled—the only way a *pure* offering could be made from the rising of the sun to its setting. But that makes the sacrifice *more* important to Christianity, not less.

· · · · · · ·

We don't know exactly when Ignatius died. If we date his martyrdom to the last part of the first century, then it's possible that the bishop of Rome at the time was Clement, another one of the Apostolic Fathers, who would shortly be martyred himself. Tradition says that St. Clement of Rome was ordained bishop by Peter himself, but different sources are divided as to whether he was bishop of Rome immediate-

---

[1] *Martyrdom of Polycarp* 41.1.

ly after Peter, or with one or two bishops in between them—
or even whether there was a single bishop of Rome at that
time, since one tradition has Peter ordaining two bishops at
once to succeed him.

Clement left one long letter that most scholars accept as
genuinely his own writing. In it he actually turns Malachi's
prophecy on its head to make his point about the unity of
the Church:

> Not in every place, brethren, are the continual daily
> sacrifices offered, or the freewill offerings, or the sin
> offerings and the trespass offerings, but in Jerusalem
> alone. And even there the offering is not made in
> every place, but before the sanctuary in the court of
> the altar; and this too through the high priest and
> the aforesaid ministers, after the victim to be offered
> has been inspected for blemishes.
>
> They therefore who do any thing contrary to
> the seemly ordinance of his will receive death as the
> penalty. You see, brethren, in proportion as greater
> knowledge has been granted to us, so much the more
> are we exposed to danger.[2]

The Old Covenant rule is that sacrifices can be offered
only in the Temple in Jerusalem. The New Testament rule,
Clement says, is still the same. But now the Temple is everywhere. It's the true Church of God, worshiping from the rising of the sun to its setting, just as Malachi told us it would.

But we still have to worship inside the Temple, not out-

---

[2] Clement of Rome, *1 Clement* 41.2–4.

side. It's vitally important not to offer the Eucharist in a way contrary to the use of the Church. It was bad enough to transgress the old laws, but now we have as our offering the body and blood of the Lord himself.

> Have we not one God and one Christ and one Spirit of grace that was shed upon us? And is there not one calling in Christ? Why do we tear and rip apart the members of Christ, and stir up factions against our own body, and reach such a pitch of folly, as to forget that we are members one of another?[3]

Here Clement is writing to the Corinthians, and we can tell that the Corinthians are still having the same problems Paul had addressed. There are still divisions, still people saying that they're *this* kind of Christian or *that* kind of Christian. However, there's only one kind of Christian, Clement insists. The Church is universal—or, to use the Greek term, catholic. You're a Christian only if you're sacrificing in the new catholic Temple with all the other Christians from the East to the West.

Clement's argument makes it clear that he thinks of the Eucharist as fulfilling in the New Covenant what Jerusalem's sacrificial cult did in the Old Covenant. And he finds a very neat way of reconciling the uniqueness of the Temple with the universality of Christianity: With the perfect sacrifice of Jesus on the cross, the single Temple at Jerusalem was not abandoned. It was suddenly enlarged to be as big as the universe.

---

[3] Clement, *1 Clement* 46.6–7.

. . . .

There's also a so-called second letter of Clement that is not a letter and almost certainly not by Clement. It's a sermon, or a motivational talk, whose subject is repenting and living the life God intends us to live as Christians. Most scholars date it to some time within a few decades before or after the year 100. It's hard to get more specific than that, although every scholar has a favorite theory. Each also has a preferred hypothesis about who wrote *Second Clement*. The best thing to say is that it's a very early Christian writing by someone who either knew the apostles or at least knew people who had known the apostles.

What's most interesting for us is how the author sees the Church in time. It's not a new thing. The Church—the real Church—is eternal and has always been there.

> Therefore, brethren, if we do the will of God, our Father, we will belong to the original Church, the spiritual Church, the Church created before the sun and moon; but if we do not do the will of the Lord, we will be among those spoken of in Scripture: "My house has become a den of robbers" (see Jeremiah 7:11). So let us choose, then, to be from the Church of life, so that we may be saved! But I don't think you don't know that the living Church is the body of Christ, for Scripture says, "God made man male and female." The male is Christ, the female the Church. And you know that the Bible and the apostles say

the Church is not just now, but from the beginning.[4]

The Church, in other words, is an eternal reality. People who do the will of God are members of the Church and always have been. It's the same Church in every time and place: the church Malachi saw in his vision, making a pure offering from the rising of the sun to its setting.

And that means Abraham was as much a member of the Church as Peter or Paul was. Once again, the Christian writer makes it clear that the Christians are the real heirs of Abraham, Moses, and David.

· · · · · · ·

The *Epistle of Barnabas*—traditionally attributed to Paul's associate Barnabas, but most likely not really by him—was probably the work of some unknown Christian writer in about the year 100. It was accepted as canonical scripture by some early churches, though it didn't make the final cut in the New Testament. The author tells us that the mistake Israel made was to emphasize the Temple as a building rather than the purpose of the building:

> Moreover, I will also tell you concerning the temple, how the wretched ones, wandering in error, trusted not in God Himself, but in the temple, as being the house of God.[5]

---

[4] Clement of Rome, *2 Clement* 14.1–2.
[5] *Barnabas* 16.1.

It was prophesied that the Temple would be destroyed, and that prophecy had come to pass in the year 70, when the Romans leveled the place at the end of the Jewish War. Now the Temple and its sacrifices were gone—or at least the physical Temple in Jerusalem was.

> Let us inquire, then, if there still is a temple of God. There is—where he himself declared he would make and finish it. . . . I find, therefore, that a temple does exist. Learn, then, how it shall be built in the name of the Lord. Before we believed in God, the habitation of our heart was corrupt and weak, as being indeed like a temple made with hands. For it was full of idolatry, and was a habitation of demons, through our doing such things as were opposed to God. But it shall be built, you observe, in the name of the Lord, in order that the temple of the Lord may be built in glory. How? Learn: having received the forgiveness of sins, and placed our trust in the name of the Lord, we have become new creatures, formed again from the beginning. For that reason in our habitation God truly dwells in us. How? His word of faith; his calling of promise; the wisdom of the statutes; the commands of the doctrine; he himself prophesying in us; he himself dwelling in us; opening to us who were enslaved by death the doors of the temple, that is, the mouth; and by giving us repentance introduced us into the incorruptible temple.[6]

---

[6] *Barnabas* 16.6–9.

Like *Clement*, the author of *Barnabas* sees that the Christians are worshiping in the real Temple. He interprets the Christians themselves as the Temple, which leads to more or less the same conclusion: the Temple is anywhere a Christian is.

. . . .

So far we have Christians writing to Christians, and perhaps to wavering Jews. But by far the largest part of the population of the Mediterranean world was pagan, and pagan philosophy was the basis of all serious education. If Christianity really was the truth for all people, Jew and Gentile, it would have to reach out to even the educated pagans. That was the obvious next step.

CHAPTER 6

THE MALACHI TEST FOR
REAL CHRISTIANS

ONE OF THE FIRST SUSTAINED ATTEMPTS by a Christian to explain the faith to philosophical pagans was a document called the *Epistle to Diognetus*.

If the *Didache* has become vanishingly rare in manuscript, the *Epistle to Diognetus* is extinct. The last known manuscript of the work was destroyed in the Franco-Prussian War in 1870. Fortunately it had been transcribed and printed several times before that.

No one knows who wrote the *Epistle to Diognetus*—though, again, every scholar has a favorite theory. The author signs himself "Mathetes," which just means "Disciple." The date is a mystery as well, but somewhere in the last half of the 100s seems to be the most popular choice among the experts. Nor does anyone know who this "Diognetus" was, who was supposed to be getting the letter: he might have been a real person, or the name might just have been picked for the sake of giving the work the literary form of a letter.

The author is keen to distinguish Christians from Jews. The Christian worship is reasonable and logical, he says, whereas the Jewish is absurd. As for the Christians, the author points out to his pagan friend that Christians are everywhere, but you might never notice them. Unlike Jews, for example, they live in the pagan world just like everybody else. They don't wear distinctive costumes; they don't eat special food; they don't separate themselves from the people around them—as Jews would have.

> But, inhabiting Greek as well as barbarian cities, as the lot of each of them has determined, and following the customs of the natives in respect to clothing, food, and the rest of their ordinary conduct, they display to us their wonderful and confessedly striking method of life. They dwell in their own countries, but simply as sojourners. As citizens, they share in all things with others, and yet endure all things as if foreigners. Every foreign land is to them as their native country, and every land of their birth as a land of strangers.[1]

This would certainly have raised some alarms with a good patriotic Roman. Who do these Christians think they are, not fitting in?

> They marry, as everyone does; they beget children, but they do not expose their offspring.[2]

This refers to the common Roman custom of leaving

---

[1] Mathetes, *Epistle to Diognetus* 5.
[2] Mathetes, *Epistle to Diognetus* 5.

unwanted babies out to die—a custom so ordinary and usual, especially if the child was a girl, that Christians were remarkable for *not* killing their children.

> They have a common table, but not a common bed. They are in the flesh, but they do not live after the flesh. They pass their days on earth, but they are citizens of heaven.[3]

So they're not good citizens—is that what you're saying? The author hastens to correct that impression. Christians are hated, but for no good reason. They're actually the best citizens you could want in your state:

> They obey the prescribed laws, and at the same time surpass the laws by their lives. They love all, and are persecuted by all. They are unknown and condemned; they are put to death, and restored to life. They are poor, yet make many rich; they lack all things, and yet abound in all; they are dishonored, and yet in their very dishonor are glorified. They are ill spoken of, and yet are justified; they are reviled, and bless; they are insulted, and repay the insult with honor; they do good, yet are punished as evildoers. When punished, they rejoice as if quickened into life; they are assailed by the Jews as foreigners, and are persecuted by the Greeks; yet those who hate them are unable to assign any reason for their hatred.[4]

[3] Mathetes, *Epistle to Diognetus* 5.
[4] Mathetes, *Epistle to Diognetus* 5.

This flight of rhetoric makes ambitious claims. But the Christian author is about to make a claim that must have seemed either wildly arrogant or mad to the ordinary pagan reader:

> To sum up everything in one word: what the soul is in the body, Christians are in the world. The soul is dispersed through all the members of the body, and Christians are scattered through all the cities of the world. The soul dwells in the body, yet is not of the body; and Christians dwell in the world, yet are not of the world. . . . The soul is imprisoned in the body, yet keeps that very body together; and Christians are confined in the world as in a prison, and yet they keep the world together.[5]

Certainly this is a daring thing to say. The Christian sect is still new—not much more than a century old—and still sparsely distributed. But it is dispersed throughout the world, in every city and town from the rising of the sun to its setting. And our unknown author is bold enough to say that these Christians are holding the world together.

That assertion might have sounded even more surprising if the pagan reader happened to know that the Christians were having a little trouble holding themselves together.

· · · · · · ·

How do you tell the real Christian Church from an

---

[5] Mathetes, *Epistle to Diognetus* 6.

impostor? It's a problem we face today, of course, when a thousand Christian sects all claim to be the real followers of Christ and all claim that every other group has it all wrong. But our time is not unique. In fact, the more we look at the early centuries of Christianity, the more they look like today.

Even Peter and Paul had to warn the Church against false teachers with wrong ideas. When Paul wrote to the Corinthians for the first time, they were already fragmented into sects.

> What I mean is that each one of you says, "I belong to Paul," or "I belong to Apollos," or "I belong to Cephas," or "I belong to Christ." Is Christ divided? Was Paul crucified for you? Or were you baptized in the name of Paul? (1 Cor 1:12–13)

But there were false teachers, too, who had to be rejected. As John says, "For many deceivers have gone out into the world, men who will not acknowledge the coming of Jesus Christ in the flesh; such a one is the deceiver and the antichrist" (2 John v. 7). The Church of the apostles, John believed, had to be on guard against people who taught false doctrines and *claimed* they were Christian.

It only got worse from there. By the mid-100s, about a century after the beginning of the Christian Church, there were dozens or possibly hundreds of Christian sects, all claiming to have the true teaching of Christ.

So how do you pick one?

As time went on there were more and more of those people. The majority always followed the teaching of the apostles, but there were splinter groups that claimed to have the real truth of Christ. The Catholic Church called them "heretics," meaning people who followed a *faction,* as opposed to people who stayed with the majority.

Judaizing Christians claimed that you still had to follow the whole Law of Moses, including circumcision, to be saved. In the opposite direction, there were "Gnostics"—people who claimed to have a secret knowledge (in Greek, *gnosis*) passed down from Jesus to a few elite followers—who claimed that the Old Testament had nothing to do with Christianity.

One of the most successful heretics was Marcion, who seems to have had ties with Gnostic teachers. He claimed that the God of the Old Testament, the one who created the world, was an inferior and evil being, and that Jesus had come to reveal the "unknown God," the good God who was really in charge of the universe. For a while these Marcionites seemed to infest the whole Roman Empire, building their own heretical churches in all the big cities. "Marcionites build churches like wasps build hives," said the Latin writer Tertullian.[6]

Tertullian was the first important Christian writer in Latin: until his time, even Christians in the Latin-speaking West wrote in Greek. He addresses both ends of the heretical spectrum in his writings, steering between the Judaizers who demanded that Christians keep the whole Law of Moses, and the Marcionites who asserted that the whole Old Testament was anti-Christian.

To the Judaizers, Tertullian's argument is that the sacrifices of the Law were a temporary concession. They were

---

[6]   Tertullian, *Against Marcion* 4.5.

never the ideal; they were there because Israel had shown itself so badly tempted by idolatry. *Fine*, said God: *you want sacrifices, I'll give you sacrifices. But they'll be done according to my instructions. That way at least you won't get into the worst kind of trouble.* And they could only be done in one place—which was the very place that now Jews, alone among all the nations, were forbidden to enter: namely Jerusalem, now the pagan city of Aelia Capitolina since the end of Bar Kokhba's revolt.[7]

Arguing against Marcion, Tertullian insists that the Old Testament prophecies make no sense unless they come from the God who will be responsible for their fulfillment. He makes distinctions like a philosopher, though unlike Justin, Tertullian claimed to have no patience for pagan philosophy.

> He thus shows that the ancient covenant is temporary only, when He indicates its change; also when He promises that it shall be followed by an eternal one. For by Isaiah He says: Hear me, and you shall live; and I will make an everlasting covenant with you, adding the sure mercies of David (Isaiah 55:3) in order that He might show that that covenant was to run its course in Christ. . . . Since, then, he said that from the Creator there would come other laws, and other words, and new dispensations of covenants, indicating also that the very sacrifices were to receive higher offices, and that among all nations,

---

[7] Marcel Simon, *Verus Israel: A Study of the Relations between Christians and Jews in the Roman Empire, AD 135–425* (London: Littman Library of Jewish Civilization, 1996), 168.

by Malachi when he says: I have no pleasure in you, says the Lord, neither will I accept your sacrifices at your hands. For from the rising of the sun, even unto the going down of the same, my name shall be great among the Gentiles; and in every place a sacrifice is offered unto my name, even a pure offering—meaning simple prayer from a pure conscience—by necessity, every change which comes as the result of innovation, introduces a diversity in those things of which the change is made, from which diversity arises also a contrariety. For as there is nothing, after it has undergone a change, which does not become different, so there is nothing different which is not contrary. Of that very thing, therefore, there will be predicated a contrariety in consequence of its diversity, to which there accrued a change of condition after an innovation. He who brought about the change was the same one who also instituted the diversity; he who foretold the innovation was likewise the same one who announced beforehand the contrariety.[8]

In this thick prose, the basic idea seems to be that any contradiction Marcion sees between the Old Testament and the New is the natural result of a change that the Old Testament God himself foretold. Malachi is the proof that the God of the Old Testament and the God of the New Testament are the same God. Why would the Old Testament God speak so plainly of the Christian worship to come if that

[8]   Tertullian, *Against Marcion* 4.1.

worship was not part of his plan?

Furthermore, Malachi's prophecy was a good test for real Christianity. In Malachi's vision, the same pure offering is made throughout the world, from the rising of the sun to its setting. Where is that actually true? Nowhere but the Catholic Church, said the Catholic Christian writers. The Eucharist is offered in every place in communion with the universal Church.

· · · · · · ·

No one spent more time thinking about how to tell real Christians from false ones than Irenaeus, bishop of Lyons in Gaul (now France). He was a bishop of the Catholic diocese there, but there were other groups that claimed to be Christian as well. Especially there were Gnostics, still claiming that they had inherited a secret teaching of Christ passed down only to the few insiders who were worthy of the knowledge.

For most of the Gnostics, who believed that the Old Testament God was a different being from the God preached by Jesus, the reason for the sacrifices of the Old Testament, was that the Old Testament God was cruel and capricious and liked lots of blood.

But Irenaeus insisted that the whole sacrificial cult of Israel was created by God for a good reason. By earthly things we could see; God showed us pictures, in them, of the heavenly things we couldn't see.

Now the gifts, offerings, and all the sacrifices were received by the people in figure, as Moses was shown on the mountain, from one and the same God whose name is now glorified in the Church among all the nations. But it makes sense that those earthly things that are spread all around us should be images of heavenly things, since they were created by the same God. For in no other way could he give us an image of the heavenly things.[9]

Because they were created by the same God, earthly things can show us images of heavenly things. And because they were created by the same God, the Temple sacrifices were not pointless exercises; they were preparing us for the perfect sacrifice to come—the one Malachi foresaw. That's clearly what Irenaeus is thinking of when he speaks of the God "whose name is now glorified in the Church among all the nations."

Sounding almost like a modern biologist, Irenaeus says that the old sacrifices and the new are the same genus, but different species:

And the genus of oblations has not been rejected; for there were oblations then, and there are oblations now: sacrifices in the people of Israel, sacrifices in the Church. But the species has been changed, since now it is offered not by slaves, but by the free. For one and the same is the Lord; the oblation of a slave, however, has its own character, as has the oblation of one who is free, so that through the oblations may be shown the indication of liberty. For nothing is

[9] Irenaeus, *Against the Heresies* 4.32.1.

useless, nothing without meaning, nothing without design when it comes to God.[10]

All the Old Testament sacrifices were necessary before we were free—and we had been slaves because we had shown, in incidents like the golden calf, that we couldn't be trusted. But this new oblation of the free, the Eucharist, offered in the new Temple of the body of Christ, is the one Malachi saw all those years ago when he gazed into the messianic age:

Again, giving directions to his disciples to offer to God the first-fruits of his own created things—not as if he stood in need of them, but that they might be themselves neither unfruitful nor ungrateful—he took that created thing, bread, and gave thanks, and said, "This is my body." And the cup likewise, which is part of that creation to which we belong, he confessed to be his blood, and taught the new oblation of the new covenant; which the Church, receiving it from the Apostles, offers to God throughout the whole world—to him who gives us for our food the first-fruits of his own gifts in the New Testament. About this, among the twelve prophets, Malachi thus foretold: "I have no pleasure in you, says the Lord of hosts, and I will not accept an offering from your hand. For from the rising of the sun to its setting my name is great among the nations, and in every place incense is offered to my name, and a pure offering; for my name is great among the nations,

---

[10] Irenaeus, *Against the Heresies* 4.31.1.

says the Lord of hosts"—meaning, quite obviously, by this that the earlier people would cease to make offerings to God; in every place, however, a sacrifice would be made to him, and that a pure one; his name is glorified among the Gentiles.

But what other name is glorified among the Gentiles than the name of our Lord, by whom the Father is glorified, and humanity also? And because it is the name of his own Son, who was made man by him, he calls it his own. Just as a king, if he himself paints a likeness of his son, is right in calling this likeness his own, both because it is of his son, and because it is his own production; so also does the Father confess the name of Jesus Christ, which is throughout all the world glorified in the Church, to be his own, both because it is that of his Son, and because he who thus describes it gave him for the salvation of men. Since, therefore, the name of the Son belongs to the Father, and since in the omnipotent God the Church makes offerings through Jesus Christ, he says well on both these grounds, "And in every place incense is offered to my name, and a pure sacrifice." Now John, in the Apocalypse, declares that the incense is the prayers of the saints.[11]

If Malachi foresaw the end of the Temple cult in Jerusalem, however, that wasn't because the Temple cult itself was a bad thing. It was created by God to lead us toward the perfect worship of the New Covenant, the offering of

---

[11] Irenaeus, *Against the Heresies* 4.29.5.

incense to God's name in every place.

. . . .

We don't know exactly when Christians began using incense in the Mass. No one unambiguously mentions using incense for most of the first three centuries, anyway. The persecutions may have made Christians wary of incense, since a pinch of incense for the pagan gods was the usual offering required to avoid martyrdom.[12] Christians don't seem to have taken up incense in their own liturgies until after the persecutions ended.

Incense seems not to have become common in the Christian world until the 400s. But even then, the "incense" in Malachi was interpreted metaphorically, usually with reference to Psalm 141:2:

Let my prayer be counted as incense before you, and
the lifting up of my hands as an evening sacrifice.

This psalm is a prayer offered in desperation: David feels defenseless unless the Lord will help him, and there is no opportunity for the external rituals of sacrifice to the Lord. He hopes his prayer will be as acceptable as incense and sacrifices would be if he had the means to offer them.

But for Irenaeus and other Christians of his time, who no longer offered any sacrifice but the Eucharist, the emphasis was turned around completely. The prayer of the Chris-

---

[12] Dom Gregory Dix, *The Shape of the Liturgy* (New York: Seabury, 1982), 426–427.

tian was the real offering. Incense, if there was any, was just the physical representation of it, a metaphor that made the prayers of the faithful visible as they rose to heaven.

> Since, therefore, the name of the Son belongs to the Father, and in the omnipotent God through Jesus Christ the Church makes its offering, it says well for both reasons, "And in every place incense is offered to me, and a pure sacrifice." But the incense, says John in Revelation, is the prayers of the saints.[13]

Irenaeus gives us what has already become the standard Christian interpretation of Malachi's prophecy. All over the world, in every place and time, Christians are sending prayers up to heaven. From the rising of the sun to its setting, there is nowhere that Christians aren't praying. This is Malachi's incense offering—not the blind, lame, and sick animals the Israelite priests had been offering on their polluted altars, the ones that made the Lord wish someone would shut the gate to the Temple, but an offering that really makes the Lord's name great among the nations.

Then why, you might ask, were there all those sacrifices in the Law of Moses? If Malachi's pure worldwide offering is a sacrifice without blood, why did God tell Moses he needed all those bloody sacrifices?

The answer, Irenaeus says, is that God prescribed those sacrifices not because he needed them, but because the people needed to make them. It was a way of luring the Israelites away from idolatry, both by giving them a feast similar to the

---

[13] Irenaeus, *Against the Heresies* 4.17.6.

ones their pagan neighbors had and by sacrificing the gods of the Egyptians on their altars:

> . . . so did the Word give to the people that very precept of making oblations, although he stood in no need of them, that they might learn to serve God.[14]

The Old Testament sacrificial cult, Irenaeus explains, was a kind of teaching tool. And we learned our lesson; we were prepared for the coming of the Messiah.

Of course, it wasn't just Irenaeus who said that. It was a message the whole Catholic Church was constantly repeating. Living in the messianic age means living in Malachi's vision.

· · · · · · ·

This prophecy would have been something you heard in church every Sunday, so important was it. Some of the Eucharistic prayers in Christian liturgies of the first few centuries make the connection to Malachi explicit. We already saw the *Didache,* from the very earliest days of the Church. There is a papyrus from the 300s or 400s that contains a Eucharistic prayer directly quoting Malachi 1:11 as part of its thanks for "this reasonable and bloodless service."[15] An anonymous writing known as the *Apostolic Constitutions* describes the whole New Covenant in terms of Malachi's pure offering:

[14] Irenaeus, *Against the Heresies* 4.31.5.

[15] Frank C. Senn, *Christian Liturgy: Catholic and Evangelical* (Minneapolis: Augsburg Fortress, 1997), 86.

He has in several ways changed the baptism ritual of the priesthood and the divine service, which was confined to one place, for instead of daily baptisms he has given only one, which is that into his death. Instead of one tribe, he has pointed out that out of every nation the best should be ordained for the priesthood; and that rather than their bodies, their religion and their lives should be examined for blemishes. Instead of a bloody sacrifice, he has appointed that reasonable and unbloody mystical one of his body and blood, which is performed to represent the death of the Lord by symbols. Instead of the divine service confined to one place, he has commanded and appointed that he should be glorified from sun rising to sun setting in every place of his dominion.[16]

For Christians, the whole Old Testament is about *us*. The meaning of it was really revealed only when Jesus Christ appeared on earth. Now everything has changed, and yet everything is the same.

A famous Christian writer called Origen, who was probably the most prolific writer of the entire classical age, tried to express the paradox in one of his sermons. Origen was a curious character. He tended toward the wildly speculative end of theology, and he came up with some ideas that were later rejected by the Church. For example, he was a universalist: he believed that the world would be recreated again and again until all beings were saved, even Satan himself. The Church rejected this idea because Scripture seems

[16] *Apostolic Constitutions* 4.23.

plainly against it and because it would deprive us of free will. What kept Origen from being a heretic was that he was always submissive to the will of the Church. He explicitly asked that the Church measure his ideas, and if they were refuted, he would accept that rejection without grumbling.

In other words, it would be heresy to teach any of Origen's incorrect ideas today, because the Church has officially pronounced on them. But Origen wasn't a heretic for suggesting them, because he honestly invited debate and was willing to be told he was wrong. So he's listed among the Church Fathers, but there's always a little asterisk by his name telling you not to believe everything he says.

While dealing with the Christian interpretation of the Old Testament—in an approved writing, of course—Origen uses paradoxical language to convey a sense of the enormous change knowing Christ makes:

> And it is astonishing that Moses is called Moses even among us and each of the prophets is addressed by his own name. For Christ did not change the names in them but the understanding. . . . He opened, therefore, the wells and taught us, that we might not seek God in some one place but might know that "sacrifice is offered to his name in every land." For it is now that time when the true worshipers worship the Father neither in Jerusalem nor on Mount Gerizim but "in spirit and in truth."[17]

Origen was living at a time when Christianity was still

---

[17] Origen, *Homilies on Genesis* 13.3.

an illegal cult in the Roman Empire. But it was spreading at an astonishing rate. Soon the Empire itself would have to come to grips with the facts: Christians made up the largest single religious group in the population. It was only a matter of time before some candidate for the imperial throne would realize that it would be a good thing to have the Christians and their God on his side. And when that happened, life would change for everyone—Christians, pagans, and Jews.

CHAPTER 7

EUSEBIUS AND THE IMPERIAL VISION

EUSEBIUS OF CAESAREA is best known today for his *Ecclesiastical History*. In fact, for most Christians it's the only thing he's known for. His *History* tells the story of how the Church went from a tiny sect to, just shortly before he wrote the book, the favored religion of the Roman Empire. Since Eusebius had access to many documents that have since been lost, the *History* preserves a good bit of early Christian writing that we wouldn't have otherwise. He was steeped in all the extant documents of the past, and he was an unusually careful historian by the standards of his time. At times he was also sympathetic to unorthodox opinions, such as those of the Arians—followers of the priest Arius who claimed that God the Son was a lesser being than the Father.

The climax of Eusebius' *History* is the victory of Constantine, the first openly Christian emperor (there were rumors about Philip the Arab), who made Christianity legal throughout the Empire and gave the Church preferential treatment, although he never did anything to make paganism illegal. In the year 324, Constantine defeated his eastern colleague Licinius, who had started to make life difficult for Christians again. As Eusebius puts it, in a flight of overblown rhetoric that was probably meant for the ears of his imperial patron:

> But Constantine, the mightiest victor, adorned with every virtue of piety—together with his son Crispus, a most God-beloved prince, and in all respects like his father—recovered the East which belonged to them; and they formed one united Roman empire as it used to be, bringing under their peaceful sway the whole world from the rising of the sun to the opposite quarter, both north and south, even to the extremities of the declining day.[1]

So Constantine's victory, in Eusebius' eyes, made Malachi's prophecy come true. The whole world was Constantine's; the whole world was Christian.

But his *History* is only one of many works Eusebius produced, and it might not have been the one he thought was most important. If you had asked him, he might have told you that the work he was proudest of was his massive two-part apologetic, *The Preparation for the Gospel* and *The Proof of the Gospel.* The first part is aimed at Gentile readers, showing how much better the Christian Scriptures are than the silly pagan myths; then the second part is meant to show how the Hebrew scriptures all pointed forward to Christ. *The Preparation* carries on the Christian argument against the pagans; *The Proof,* the argument against the Jews. In both

---

[1] Eusebius, *Ecclesiastical History* 10.9.6.

he's very big on the proof from prophecy: the idea that we know the Gospel is true because the prophets foretold it so long ago.

Eusebius contrasts the Christians with "the circumcision"—Jews who still observed the Law of Moses. Again, it's important to point out that this isn't anything to do with race or nationality. There are Jews and Gentiles who have accepted Christ, and they're equally part of the New Covenant. It's an argument about theology, and a bitter one, but Eusebius isn't trying to get rid of his opponents. He doesn't want Jews to disappear. Instead, he's trying to make them see things his way, so they can be part of the New Covenant like him.

For Eusebius, as we already saw, Christ was talking about Malachi's prophecy—and the other Old Testament prophets who spoke of the end of the Temple cult—when he told the Samaritan woman that a time was coming when worship would be neither at Jerusalem nor at Mt. Gerizim, the Samaritans' holy place. After quoting Malachi 1:10–11, he explains it as referring to the Christians' lives:

> By the incense and offering to be offered to God in every place, what else can he mean but that no longer in Jerusalem nor exclusively in that place, but in every land and among all nations they will offer to the Supreme God the incense of prayer and the sacrifice called "pure," because it is not a sacrifice of blood but of good works?[2]

---

[2] Eusebius, *Proof of the Gospel* 1.6.19c.

In Eusebius' eyes, the Eucharist is part of that sacrifice of good works. In fact, it's the summation of all the good works Christians offer to God. The Jewish sacrifices were "symbols and images," but the truth isn't really in them: "we do not reckon it right to fall back on the first beggarly elements, which are symbols and images but do not contain the truth itself."[3] The Eucharist is a symbol, but not merely a symbol. It is a sacrament: it really is what it represents.

> While then the better, the great and worthy and divine sacrifice was not yet available for humanity, it was necessary for them to pay a ransom for their own life by offering animals. And, appropriately, this was a life that represented their own nature. That was what the holy men of old did. They anticipated by the Holy Spirit that a holy victim, dear to God and great, would one day come for humanity, as the offering for the sins of the world. They believed that as prophets they must perform in symbol his sacrifice, and display in an image what was yet to be. But when that which was perfect had come, in accordance with the predictions of the prophet, as the prophets had predicted, the former sacrifices ceased at once because of the better and true Sacrifice.[4]

Later, Eusebius quotes Malachi's prophecy again and explains in detail what he thinks the pure sacrifice is:

[3] Eusebius, *Proof of the Gospel* 1.37c.
[4] Eusebius, *Proof of the Gospel* 1.36b–c.

We sacrifice, therefore, to Almighty God a sacrifice of praise. We sacrifice the divine and holy and sacred offering. We sacrifice anew according to the new covenant the pure sacrifice. But the sacrifice to God is called "a contrite heart." "A broken and contrite heart, O God, you will not despise" (Psalm 51:17). Yes, and we offer the incense of the prophet, in every place bringing him the sweet-smelling fruit of the sincere Word of God, offering it in our prayers to him. This yet another prophet teaches, who says, "Let my prayer be counted as incense before you" (Psalm 141:2).

So, then, we sacrifice and offer incense, on the one hand, when we celebrate the memorial of his great sacrifice according to the mysteries he delivered to us, and bring to God the Eucharist for our salvation with holy hymns and prayers; while on the other hand we consecrate ourselves to him alone and to the Word his High Priest, devoted to him body and soul. Therefore we are careful to keep our bodies pure and undefiled from all evil, and we bring our hearts purified from every passion and stain of sin, and worship him with sincere thoughts, real intention, and true beliefs. For these are more acceptable to him (as we are taught) than a multitude of sacrifices offered with blood and smoke and fat.

However, the prophecy of Malachi didn't just predict the coming of the Christians' perfect sacrifice. According to Eusebius, it also predicted the rejection of the Jews. And here, once again, is where we get ourselves into a mess if we're not careful. With so many centuries of persecution of the Jews behind us, it's easy to read Christian writings of the 300s through the filter of Nazi writings of the 1930s. We have to keep reminding ourselves of the fundamental difference.

For the Nazis, what was wrong with the Jews was their race. It couldn't be fixed. There was no way to change a Jew so that he wasn't a Jew, and in the mad world of Nazi race theory that was enough to disqualify every Jew—even the ones who had become Christian generations ago—from being really human.

But for Eusebius and other Christians of his time, what was wrong with the Jews was that they believed the wrong things. Show them why they were wrong—by appealing to the same scriptures they accepted as the revealed word of God—and they could stop being wrong. That was the purpose of the most confrontational Christian writings: not to condemn the Jews as a people but to make them see how wrong they were about the Scriptures.

So when Eusebius quotes Malachi again as a "rebuke of the Jewish people,"[5] what he means is that Malachi, like many prophets before him, was telling the people that they were doing the wrong things because they believed the wrong things. They believed the sacrifices in the Law of Moses were the ends, but they were only the means. The thing God really wants is a pure heart.

Thus the prophecies about the coming of Christ

not only foretold that good things for the nations would be associated with the date of his appearance,

5 Eusebius, *Proof of the Gospel* 1.56a.

but also the reverse for the Jews. Yes, the Hebrew oracles foretell distinctly the fall and ruin of the Jewish race through their disbelief in Christ, so that we [the Gentiles who have accepted Christ] should no longer appear equal to them, but better than they.[6]

Eusebius is one of the many commentators who sees Jesus as referring to Malachi when he tells the Samaritan woman that "the hour is coming, and now is, when the true worshipers will worship the Father in spirit and truth" (John 4:23). Eusebius quotes this passage and adds,

So he said—and soon, not long after, Jerusalem was besieged, the holy place and the altar beside it and the worship conducted according to Moses' laws were destroyed, and the archetypal holiness of the men of God before Moses reappeared. And the blessing assured thereby to all nations came, to lead those who came to it away from the first step and from the first elements of the Mosaic worship toward a better and more perfect life. Yes, the religion of those blessed and godly men—who did not worship in any one place exclusively, either by symbols or by types, but as our Lord and Savior requires "in spirit and in truth"—by our Savior's appearance became the possession of all the nations, as the prophets of old foresaw.[7]

---

[6] Eusebius, *Proof of the Gospel* 1.53a.
[7] Eusebius, *Proof of the Gospel* 1.6.

And then, of course, he quotes Malachi as foreseeing it.

. . . .

As is typical, Eusebius was not alone in his interpretation of Malachi's prophecy as rejecting Judaism in favor of Christianity. One of Constantine's other Christian friends was Lactantius, a distinguished Christian writer who offered very much the same interpretation:

> On account of these impieties of theirs he cast them off forever, and so he ceased to send to them prophets. But he commanded his own Son, the first-begotten, the maker of all things, his own counselor, to descend from heaven, so that he might transfer the sacred religion of God to the Gentiles—that is, to those who were ignorant of God—and might teach them righteousness, which the perfidious people had cast aside. And he had long before threatened that he would do this, as the prophet Malachi shows, saying: "I have no pleasure in you, says the Lord, and I will not accept an offering from your hands; for from the rising of the sun even unto its setting, my name shall be great among the Gentiles."[8]

In another place, he piles up several quotations from the prophets to prove the same point. One of the quotations, of course, is from Malachi:

---

[8] Lactantius, *Divine Institutes* 4.11.

Now, that the Jews were disinherited, because they rejected Christ, and that we, who are of the Gentiles, were adopted into their place, is proved by the Scriptures. Jeremiah thus speaks: "I have forsaken my house, I have given my heritage into the hands of her enemies. My heritage has become to me as a lion in the forest; it has given forth its voice against me: therefore have I hated it" (Jeremiah 12:7–8). Also Malachi: "I have no pleasure in you, says the Lord, neither will I accept an offering at your hand. For from the rising of the sun even unto the going down thereof, my name shall be great among the Gentiles."[9]

Lactantius alludes to Malachi again when he talks about the Crucifixion:

Lastly, no nation is so uncivilized, no region so remote, that either his passion or the height of his majesty would be unknown. Therefore in his suffering he stretched forth his hands and measured out the world, so that even then he might show that a great multitude, collected together out of all languages and tribes, from the rising of the sun even to his setting, was about to come under his wings, and to receive on their foreheads that great and lofty sign.[10]

What greater multitude could there be than the entire

---

[9] Lactantius, *Epitome of the Divine Institutes* 48.
[10] Lactantius, *Divine Institutes* 4.26.

Roman Empire itself? From the Roman point of view, the Empire and the world were practically the same thing. There were a few barbarians outside, but the best and most populous parts of the earth belonged to Rome. And new Christians were still coming into the Church. It seemed inevitable that, sooner or later, the whole Empire would be Christian, from the rising of the sun to its setting.

Of course, there was an awful temptation to help the process along a little.

CHAPTER 8

JOHN CHRYSOSTOM AND THE JEWISH QUESTION

UNDER CONSTANTINE, the law was liberty for all religions. But under his sons the Roman Empire began to slide back toward intolerance—this time in the other direction. Now pagans and Jews were suffering the persecution. It was seldom violent, but it was certainly inconvenient at the least.

In the year 357, Constantius proclaimed an edict that made it illegal to convert from Christianity to Judaism:

> If anyone, after renouncing the venerated Christian faith, should become a Jew, and join their sacrilegious assemblies, We order that, after the accusation has been proved, his property shall be confiscated to the Treasury. Given at Milan, on the fifth of the Nones of July, during the Consulate of Constantius, Consul for the ninth time, and Julian-Cæsar, Consul for the second time, 357.[1]

---

[1] Constantius, *Codex Justinian* 1.7.1.

This law is interesting partly because it shows Christians abusing their power. (The emperors were always happy to find another crime for which they could decree that "his property shall be confiscated to the Treasury," for pretty obvious reasons.) But it's most interesting because it shows that the line between Christianity and Judaism was still fuzzier than either ancient or modern writers would have us believe. Laws like this are enacted only when somebody identifies a problem. There must have been Christians converting to Judaism, and it must have happened often enough that Constantius thought there needed to be a law against it—or often enough that Constantius thought the confiscations would make a useful addition to the imperial treasury, which comes to the same thing. Conversions were happening, and the emperor noticed. We'll see plenty of other evidence of this fuzzy line.

Incidentally, the Julian Caesar who co-signed the edict was Constantius' young cousin, recently elevated to junior emperor—later to be known as "Julian the Apostate," the emperor who tried to drag the Roman Empire back to paganism. At the time of this edict, he was a Christian to all appearances, but it seems his philosophical education had already poisoned his mind against Christianity—or having Constantius as an example had done it, since Constantius had murdered most of Julian's family, leaving Julian only because he was young and harmless. If that's what a Christian is like, who wants to be one?

So here's the situation as the 300s progress: except for a brief and completely unsuccessful reversion to paganism from 361 to 363, the Roman Empire is officially Christian, and other religions are more and more suppressed. The ones who suffer most are the Christians who are the wrong kind of Christian. For a while the Arians have the ear of the emperor, and the Catholic majority is oppressed. Then the Catholics come back into power, and the Arians and other heretical groups are afflicted. Pagans and Jews probably suffer less than the wrong kinds of Christians, because the debates with them aren't as interesting to the Catholic majority right now.

But that doesn't mean there aren't arguments. And those between Christians and Jews are usually far more bitter than the ones between Christians and pagans, because Christians and Jews share a tradition that pagans still don't understand.

One of the most famous of the Fathers carried on that argument with even more vigor than usual. As a result, he's earned a reputation as one of the worst "anti-Semites" among all the Christian writers. But let's try to understand what he was up to.

· · · · · · ·

They called him the Man with the Golden Mouth. That's what "Chrysostom" means, and St. John Chrysostom earned that title by being the most mesmerizing preacher in the East.

John came from Antioch, where in the late 300s he began to earn his golden-mouthed reputation as a priest who preached sermons that everyone talked about.

Antioch was a lively place, in both good and bad ways. We've already met St. Ignatius, who was bishop of Antioch two hundred years before John Chrysostom started to become famous. By John's time, Constantinople and fast-growing Milan had been added to the list of great cities of the

Roman Empire. But Antioch was still a very important place, especially as a center of Christian culture. It was, after all, the place where Christians were first called Christians, and we can presume that no Christian from Antioch would ever let you forget that.

The people of Antioch were prone to public displays of enthusiasm, and sometimes those displays turned into riots. In one notorious case, a protest against new taxes erupted into a rampage that left the statues of the emperor and his family toppled and smashed. Those statues were the imperial presence itself; whatever was done to them was done to the imperial household, and the penalty would be just as severe. When the people of Antioch woke up with a monumental hangover the next morning, they realized they were in deep, deep trouble.

This was where John Chrysostom's reputation was really sealed. Over the next few days, as the people waited, trembling, for word of what horrible punishment the emperor would inflict—loss of the city charter? leveling the city? general massacre?—John preached a series of utterly memorable sermons that kept the people calm. It was a time for repentance, he told them, but also a time of hope. And in fact, while John was preaching, his bishop was off pleading with the emperor, and fortunately the emperor was persuaded. He was satisfied with the punishment of the people who had toppled the statues, or at least who were accused of toppling them; these people had already been executed by the local authorities. As for the rest, the emperor was happy to show them his mercy.

It was an extreme example, perhaps, but it was the sort of thing that happened in Antioch all the time. Violence might easily be seething under the smooth facade of culture.

Antioch also had a large Jewish population with a lively culture of its own. It was a great and prosperous community; new synagogues were still being built in the area.[2] And that is where John saw a problem. Christians and Jews were neighbors, friends, and relatives, and they were invited to each other's parties. Many Christians would end up going to Jewish feasts and probably think nothing of it.

But there seems to have been a lot of conversion going on in both directions. There were Christians who, having been to the Jewish feasts, probably became convinced that the Old Testament rites were still necessary. They became "Judaizers"—Christians who followed Jewish customs and insisted that those customs were needed for salvation. Some of them would go further and renounce Christ completely.

So John preached another famous series of sermons, this time against the Jews. And because of them St. John Chrysostom is often accused of being one of the worst anti-Semites among the Fathers of the Church—and if you were to read his writings without understanding anything about the context, you'd probably agree with that assessment. He calls the Jews all kinds of names. He says he hates them. He accuses them of having killed Jesus, a thing that happened three hundred years before any of the Jews he knew were born. Isn't that anti-Semitic?

Well, it's complicated.

First of all, we have to remember once again that he's not talking about a race. Even when he refers to the "na-

---

[2] Robert L. Wilken, *John Chrysostom and the Jews* (Eugene, OR: Wipf and Stock, 1983), 56.

tion" of the Jews, Chrysostom is condemning an *opinion*.
Jews can become Christians, and then they cease to be Jews.
And Christians can become Jews too. That was what really worried Chrysostom. The separation between Jews and
Christians was far from complete. They had too many things
in common. The pagans had different traditions, and it was
easy to see where the line was that separated Christianity
from paganism. But Christianity and Judaism were still two
sides of the same coin, sharing the same ancient tradition
and each claiming to be the real heir of Abraham and Moses.

Second, we have to remember that Chrysostom doesn't
use any worse language for Jews than he does for other
Christians—if they're the wrong kind of Christian. The
strong language he does use is the language of rhetoric.

Preaching was very different in the late 300s from what
it is today. It was one of the chief forms of public entertainment. It attracted the same kind of audience the theater might attract. People crowded around the preacher and
clapped and shouted when he made a point they liked. Or
they booed him if he was boring. So he'd better not be boring.[3]

Chrysostom was never boring.

Furthermore, when we look at the occasion of the notorious sermons that tarnish Chrysostom's reputation today, we come to a very interesting conclusion. Chrysostom's
sermons aren't evidence of some pervasive anti-Semitism
in Antioch—in fact, they're exactly the reverse. They make
it obvious that Christians and Jews in Antioch were really
very friendly. A little *too* friendly, Chrysostom thought. He

[3] Wilken, *John Chrysostom*, 105.

was worried about his congregation joining the "Judaizing" faction of Christianity, at a time when that was still a very real possibility. Within the Church, there were very active Judaizers—active and perhaps persuasive. Especially in the East, the Fathers were often fretting about the attraction of Jewish customs. They wouldn't have worried about it if it wasn't happening. And there's some evidence that the Judaizing tendency was gaining strength in Chrysostom's time.[4]

The Saint's famous intervention in the argument started in about the year 380, when in the middle of preaching a series of sermons on the Anomoean heresy—an extreme form of Arianism—Chrysostom suddenly changed topics. One morning his congregation showed up expecting to hear more about the Anomoeans and found John ready to preach about the Jews instead. It was the first of what would be a series of sermons "Against the Jews"—but really against Christians who adopted Jewish customs and theology. No Jews were listening; we can be fairly confident that not many Jews would have shown up at a Christian church to hear a sermon against the Anomoean heresy.

And it's very interesting to hear the reason for John's sudden change of topic: The Anomoeans are outside the Church; we apparently don't have to worry about any immediate danger from them. But the Jewish danger is right here inside the Church. It affects our own Catholic members.

> But what shall we do? Another illness, the gravest imaginable, demands all our attention. We are speaking of an illness that affects the very body of

4 Wilken, *John Chrysostom*, 70–73.

the Church. We must cure it before anything else; the sick outside the church will come afterward. Our first care ought to be for those of our family; strangers have a right to our care only after that.

But what is this illness? The feasts of those miserable Jews are about to arrive—continual and incessant feasts: trumpets, tabernacles, fasts—and many of those who share the same society with us, who claim that they have the same thoughts we have, attend those feasts. Some go to see them; others even take part in them, and observe the Jewish fasts.

It is this perverse custom from which I now wish to rescue the Church. For the discourse against the Anomoeans can be put off to another time without your suffering at all from the delay; but it is to be feared that some of our brethren who have come down with the Jewish disease, if we do not give them our attention now that the feasts of the Jews are near, may, owing to bad habit and great ignorance, participate in their iniquities, and then what good will our speeches be? In fact, if they are not warned today, they will fast with the Jews, and when the sin has been committed, it will be in vain to apply the remedy. That is why I hasten to get there in time.[5]

From this we learn what the real "illness" is. It's not that the Christians and the Jews have separated. In Chrysostom's opinion, it's that they haven't separated nearly enough. The Jewish feasts are coming, and he knows that some of the

[5] John Chrysostom, *Homilies Against the Jews* 3.1.1.

people in his own congregation will be going with their Jewish friends to celebrate them.

Why is that such a bad thing? What's wrong with celebrating the Old Testament festivals, even if you're a Christian? Aren't they part of our heritage? Apparently the Jewish population of Antioch make these feasts into big occasions, because Chrysostom knows that a fair number of Christians will be going just to watch without participating. There must be something to see, and what's wrong with that?

The answer must be that the Christians who go are exposing themselves to danger, at least in the eyes of Chrysostom. There's a chance they might become Judaizers—Christians who believe that the Jewish ceremonies are necessary for salvation. Or, worse, they might turn their backs on Christ and become Jews. Chrysostom tries to make his flock see Christianity and Judaism as two completely separate things; then he asks, *why do Christians celebrate with Jews if Jews don't celebrate with Christians?*

> When have you seen them observing the paschal fast? When have they celebrated the feast of the martyrs with us? When have they joined with us for the day of Epiphany? They do not rush toward the truth, and you—you rush toward iniquity. I say *iniquity* because their fasts are not done at the right time. There was a time when it was necessary to observe them as they observe them. But that time is no more. That is why what was then conformable to the divine law has now become contrary to it.[6]

---

[6] John Chrysostom, *Homilies Against the Jews* 4.3.9.

By participating in Jewish festivals, a Christian is as good as saying that the Incarnation never happened, the Messiah never came.

If Chrysostom was afraid of the Jewish festivals, he probably had good reasons. We saw how the edict of Constantius and Julian suggested that the lines between Judaism and Christianity were still very fuzzy and easy to cross. Christians must have been converting to Judaism—probably not in huge numbers, but still often enough to make the leaders of the Church worried. They had seen it happen.

So when Christian writers of the time, like John Chrysostom, emphasize the separation between Christians and Jews, they're emphasizing it precisely because it's not *real* enough yet. They're reinforcing the idea that Jews are different from Christians, because recognizably, they're part of the same tradition.

As John's unexpected sermon against the Jews turned into a whole series of sermons, he used the rhetorical trick of pretending to address his opponents directly. But remember that he's not really talking to Jews; he's talking to the Christians in his own church. He doesn't really expect to convince Jews with his arguments, and he's not trying, because there are no Jews in his audience. These are arguments aimed at Christians who might be tempted toward the Judaizing heresy.

And of course the strongest argument John can think of against Judaizing comes from our favorite prophet:

> Listen to Malachi, who came after the other prophets; for I shall not produce the testimony either of Isaiah, or of Jeremiah, or of the others who preceded

the captivity, for fear that you should tell me that the evils they announced happened in the captivity. I produce a prophet who, after the return from Babylon and the rebuilding of Jerusalem, clearly predicted what concerns you.

When the Jews had returned, had recovered their city, rebuilt their Temple, and started up their sacrifices again, Malachi, in announcing their coming destruction and the abolition of their sacrifices, speaks to them in this way in the person of God: "I will not accept your victims, says the Lord of hosts; for from the rising of the sun to its setting my name is great among the nations; in every place incense is burned before me, and a pure sacrifice is offered to me; but you have profaned it."

When is it, ye Jews, that this prediction was fulfilled? When is it that incense was burned in every place before the Lord? When was a pure sacrifice offered to him?

You cannot cite any other time than after the coming of Jesus Christ.

If the prophet speaks not of the present time and of our sacrifice, but of yours, the prophecy will contradict the law. For if, though Moses commands that sacrifice be offered nowhere but the place chosen by the Lord; if, though he confines the sacrifices to a single location, the prophet says that incense should be burned in every place, and a pure sacrifice offered, he is struggling with the law of Moses; he is against it. But there is no struggle between them, no contradiction. Moses speaks of one sacrifice, and Malachi of another. And what proves it? What we have just said, and many other proofs besides.

First, the place itself. He predicted that this worship would not be confined to a single city, as it was under the Jews, but that it would extend from the rising of the sun to its setting.

Then the nature of the sacrifice: in calling it "pure," he announces which sacrifice he is talking about.

Finally, the persons who offer it: he does not say in Israel, but among all the nations. And so that you may not suppose that this worship should be limited to one or two cities, he does not say simply in every place, but from the rising of the sun to its setting, meaning that the Gospel would be preached in every place where the sun shines.

He says that the new sacrifice will be *pure*, as if the old one had been impure, not in itself, but because of the disposition of those who offered it. About which he said, "Incense is an abomination to me" (Isaiah 1:13). And what St. Paul said about the law and grace, that the law has no real splendor when we compare it to the sublimity of the Gospel (see 2 Corinthians 3:10), we may repeat here with assurance: we may say that the new sacrifice is the only pure one, if we compare it to the old; for it is offered not with the smoke and odor of victims, nor with the blood and price of redemption, but by the grace of the Holy Spirit.[7]

---

[7]   John Chrysostom, *Homilies Against the Jews* 5.12.3.

This is a very detailed argument for the Christian interpretation of Malachi. What it boils down to is this: Malachi can't be talking about Jewish worship, because he talks about a sacrifice offered from one end of the world to the other; and it's not a bloody sacrifice with burning fat but a *pure* sacrifice.

And we can tell that it's not an argument really addressed to the Jews. Speaking to the Jews is a rhetorical technique. This is a sermon preached to Christians. It's telling them why they're right.

A French scholar of the late 1800s, Ernest Renan, looked at Chrysostom's sermons against the Jews and saw a vivid picture of Jewish and Christian communities in Antioch intertwined almost inextricably. He didn't like Chrysostom very much, it seems, but as a picture of life in his time he found the *Discourses Against the Jews* fascinating:

> One feels that the separation is in process of accomplishment, but it only becomes in a manner complete when Christianity becomes a State religion under Constantine. Then Christianity becomes official, while Judaism retains its liberal character. Is the separation at last complete? Oh, no, not yet.
>
> I lately referred to the sermons of St. John Chrysostom against the Jews. There is no historical document more interesting. The author naturally shows himself rude, dogmatic; he makes all sorts of arguments, some of them not very strong. But one sees that the faithful are still in a community of people most intimate with the synagogue. He tells them more than twenty times (for St. John Chrysostom

repeats himself a good deal, he is rather prolix), "What have you to do at the synagogue? You wish to celebrate the Passover? Well, we also celebrate the Passover; come to us."

In 380, then, the Christians of Antioch used to go to synagogue on several occasions. In order to make an oath more binding, people went to the synagogue, because the sacred books were there. Here, to tell the truth, is the cause of the custom which John Chrysostom combats as one of the gravest abuses. "I know well," says Chrysostom, "what you are going to tell me. You will say that the Law and the Prophets are there." The Christians did not sufficiently practice the Hebrew Bible, and they felt that the Jews were its true guardians.[8]

Christians were ignorant of their own scriptural heritage, and so they were attracted to the synagogues and the Jewish customs.

. . . .

Chrysostom's *Discourses Against the Jews* is notorious today, and it doesn't help that it's hard to find in English. If you look for these writings on the Internet, you're likely to end up at some weird anti-Semitic conspiracy-theory site.

But both the people who condemn Chrysostom and

---

[8] Ernest Renan, quoted in the *Jewish Literary Annual* (London: Union of Jewish Literary Societies, 1904), 24. The Chrysostom passage is from *Homilies Against the Jews* 1.5.2.

the people who try to press him into service as a Jew-hater are missing the context. These sermons are part of the long argument between Christians and Jews that was still very much going on in the late 300s. Furthermore, Chrysostom's rhetoric against Jews is mild compared to his rhetoric against heretical Christians.

Anti-Semitism would come later, and it would be horrifying. But this was a family squabble.

And Malachi would find himself dragged into it at every opportunity.

CHAPTER 9

A Couple of Cyrils

Two men named Cyril joined the ranks of the great Christian thinkers of the late 300s, and of course they both thought quite a bit about Malachi's famous prophecy.

St. Cyril of Jerusalem is another on the long list of Christian writers who point to Malachi as predicting not only the Eucharistic celebrations of the universal Church but also the downfall of Judaism:

> But after the Jews for the plots which they made against the Savior were cast away from His grace, the Savior built out of the Gentiles a second Holy Church, the Church of us Christians, concerning which he said to Peter, And upon this rock I will build My Church, and the gates of hell shall not prevail against it (Matthew 16:18). And David prophesying of both these, said plainly of the first which was rejected, I have hated the Congregation of evil doers; but of the second which is built up he says in the same Psalm, Lord, I have loved the

beauty of Your house; and immediately afterwards, In the Congregations will I bless you, O Lord. For now that the one Church in Judea is cast off, the Churches of Christ are increased over all the world; and of them it is said in the Psalms, Sing unto the Lord a new song, His praise in the Congregation of Saints. Agreeably to which the prophet also said to the Jews, I have no pleasure in you, says the Lord Almighty (Malachi 1:10); and immediately afterwards, For from the rising of the sun even unto the going down of the same, My name is glorified among the Gentiles.[1]

Here's another example of the Fathers' argument that the Jews were "cast off" in favor of the Christians. Once again, we have to remember the context. The proposition would be picked up in the Middle Ages as an excuse for horrible violence against Jews, and grinding oppression when there wasn't open violence. But that would be much later. Right now, in Cyril of Jerusalem's time, the argument is simply an argument.

The *Apostolic Constitutions,* a document usually dated to the third century, gives us what looks like an updated version of the instructions from the *Didache:*

On the day of the resurrection of the Lord—that is, the Lord's day—assemble yourselves together, without fail, giving thanks to God, and praising him for those mercies God has bestowed upon you through

---

[1] Cyril of Jerusalem, *Catechetical Lectures* 18.25.

Christ, and has delivered you from ignorance, error, and bondage, that your sacrifice may be unspotted, and acceptable to God, who has said concerning his universal Church: "In every place shall incense and a pure sacrifice be offered unto me; for I am a great King, says the Lord Almighty, and my name is wonderful among the heathen."[2]

Viewing the Eucharist as the perfect sacrifice in Malachi would have been familiar to Christians all over the Roman Empire from liturgies and homilies. They would all have heard that it fulfilled all the sacrifices of the Old Testament, which were only imperfect images of the perfect Eucharist that was to come.

Of course, this would have provoked an argument from Jewish listeners. And there were some parts of the world where Christians would have heard the Jewish arguments loudly and often. Antioch was one of those places, but Alexandria even more.

· · · · · · ·

Antioch could be a violent place, but Alexandria made it look like an old folks' home. The characteristic social gathering in Alexandria was the mob. In this intellectual center of the Roman Empire, angry mobs would take up abstruse philosophical slogans the way English football hooligans gather around their teams.

By the early 400s, Alexandria was divided into three main

---

[2] *Apostolic Constitutions* 7.30.

mobs (not to mention innumerable sub-mobs): the Christians, the Pagans, and the Jews. Christianity was by now the official religion of the Roman Empire, but many influential pagans still practiced the old religion—or at least disdained to practice Christianity. And the Jewish population had always been large and important in the city: Alexandria was where the Septuagint, the standard Greek translation of the Old Testament, had been made, and it was full of Jewish intellectual activity. Now that Jerusalem was no longer Jewish (although Jews had been moving back since Constantine took over), Alexandria had become the cultural center of the Jewish world.

The mobs may have been about equally divided, but the privileged position of the Christian religion made the bishop's office one of the most important positions in the city. In fact, it may have been *the* most important. At any rate, it was a prize worth fighting over, and Alexandria loved a good fight. When the old bishop Theophilus died in 412, the election turned into the expected bloody riots. When the dust had settled, Theophilus' nephew Cyril was bishop.

Cyril found himself head of a tremendously wealthy church and also—whether he liked it or not—the de facto leader of a violent mob. The Church certainly did a lot of good in Alexandria: it had set up a system of medical care for the poor that would have been the envy of most developed cities today, and Christian ambulance squads prowled the streets actually looking for people who needed help. But if someone started shouting a slogan, the ambulance squads could turn into violent thugs.

In the most notorious incident, a Christian mob murdered Hypatia, a woman who had the distinction of being practically the only notable female philosopher in ancient history. They seem to have thought that she was behind some bad blood between Cyril and the Roman governor. Modern legend—going back to a popular novel called *Hypatia* by Charles Kingsley—makes Cyril the villain in this riot, but he was probably just as helpless as any other authorities once the mob got moving.

Calmer Christian minds of the time were horrified. The Christian historian Socrates Scholasticus is the one who tells us about the incident, and he says it brought shame on Cyril and the entire Alexandrian church. But the shame was that Cyril couldn't control the mob, not that he incited the riot. Even the Roman governor who hated him didn't blame Cyril for the murder.[3]

The Hypatia affair shows what Alexandria was in those days: a seething cauldron of incipient violence, just waiting for some trifling incident to boil over into murder.

· · · · · · ·

Cyril of Alexandria is another important Christian figure often accused of anti-Semitism. But once again, we have to remember the context. His sermons, like John Chrysostom's, were vigorous and confrontational precisely because people were crossing lines easily. As always, it's not a question of race: it's an argument about ideas. For Cyril, a Christian who celebrated the Jewish feasts was denying the central truth of

---

[3] Lionel R. Wickham, "Cyril of Alexandria," in *Encyclopedia of Early Christianity*, ed. Everett Ferguson (New York: Garland, 1999), 310–311.

Christianity: that the old sacrifices had been fulfilled in one perfect worldwide sacrifice.

> The Law, you see, was a prefiguring and foretelling of worship in spirit and in truth, and "regulations for the body," as the divinely inspired Paul writes, "until the time comes to set things right." Now, the time for reform would, in my view, be no other than the coming of our Savior. . . . Accordingly, he clearly told those exercising priesthood according to the Law that they are unacceptable to him or, rather, *I have no pleasure in them* as they perform sacrifices in shadow and type, and that he would *not accept* what was offered by them.[4]

Because the old sacrifices were shadows and types, they are not acceptable once we've reached the time when the *real* sacrifice is offered—the time after the coming of Jesus Christ.

This theme was one of Cyril of Alexandria's obsessions. His first exegetical work was *Adoration and Worship of God in Spirit and in Truth*, in which he explains what it means when Jesus says, "Think not that I have come to abolish the law and the prophets; I have come not to abolish them but to fulfil them. For truly, I say to you, till heaven and earth pass away, not an iota, not a dot, will pass from the law until all is accomplished" (Matt 5:17–18).

---

[4] Cyril of Alexandria, *Commentary on Malachi* 1, in *Commentary on the Twelve Prophets*, tr. Robert Hill (Washington, DC: Catholic University of America, 2013), 298.

If that is true, then why aren't we still following the whole Law of Moses? Because Jesus also said, "But the hour is coming, and now is, when the true worshipers will worship the Father in spirit and truth" (John 4:23). The Christian way of worship is worship in spirit and in truth: the law in the Old Testament was a shadow, an image, of that reality. Thus, when we celebrate the Christian sacrifice, we're celebrating the *reality* represented by the Law of Moses.[5]

Modern writers sometimes charge Cyril with anti-Semitism—and again it's certainly true that his words were taken up and used in the service of vicious hatred later on. But in his time he was insisting on a principle. If Christianity means anything at all, then it means that the Old Testament sacrifices are all wrapped up in the Christian Eucharist. From the rising of the sun to its setting, Malachi's pure offering is going on in the Christian churches. To return to the law would be to return to slavery; Christians are free, and they ought to stay that way.

All these arguments depend on a particularly Christian reading of the Old Testament. To be a Christian was to believe that the Old Testament was making the paths straight for the ultimate coming of the Christ. To make these arguments, then, you had to have a good knowledge of the Hebrew Scriptures.

Every famous Church Father of the time was convinced that knowing the Old Testament was tremendously important for any Christian who pretended to know anything about the faith. And there was no one who knew the Old Testa-

---

[5] Robert L. Wilken, *Judaism and the Early Christian Mind* (New Haven: Yale University Press, 1971), 69–71.

ment better than St. Jerome, who learned Hebrew so that he could read it in the original and who gave the Latin-speaking Church the Vulgate, the standard Latin translation of the Bible.

. . . .

In a letter to Paulinus, bishop of Nola, Jerome tells his correspondent that knowledge of Scripture is one of the most important things a bishop can have. "It is idle to try to teach what you do not know, and—if I may speak with some warmth—is worse still to be ignorant of your ignorance."[6] So he goes through the whole Bible, giving Paulinus a capsule summary of each book. And when he gets to Malachi, the one thing he considers essential to know about the book is the prophecy in Malachi 1:10–11:

> Malachi, the last of all the prophets, speaks openly of the rejection of Israel and the calling of the nations. "I have no pleasure in you, says the Lord of hosts, neither will I accept an offering at your hand. For from the rising of the sun even unto the going down of the same, my name is great among the Gentiles: and in every place incense is offered unto my name, and a pure offering."[7]

This is what a Christian bishop needs to know: that Malachi foretold the Church, and also the rejection of Juda-

---

[6] Jerome, *Letters* 53.7.
[7] Jerome, *Letters* 53.8.

ism. As Jerome sees it, those are the two prongs of Malachi's prophecy: salvation has come to the world through the Jews, but the Jewish rites have been rejected now that the pure offering is established from the rising of the sun to its setting. This is a very neat summary of how most of the Christian writers of Jerome's time see Malachi's vision. It's a vision of the Eucharist but also a vision of the parting of the ways. Whoever clings to the old customs will be left behind.

Following suit, Jerome is yet another Father often accused of anti-Semitism, so it's worth remembering what he did to become the greatest Scripture scholar of his age. He went to Judea and attached himself to Jewish rabbis, who taught him to read and speak Hebrew fluently (although he never quite managed to speak it without an accent). Day after day he sat in their company, poring over the Hebrew Scriptures, listening as they corrected his elementary mistakes.

In other words, he was not an anti-Semite. He was close friends with some very religious Jews. But he did not agree with them about religion. They knew it. And he knew that they did not agree with him. There were arguments to be had—vigorous arguments. But that didn't mean they couldn't be friends.

Jerome's interpretation of Malachi—that Malachi saw both the Eucharist and the parting of the ways between the people of the New Covenant and the people of the Old—is the same interpretation we would see in the most famous Christian theologian of all, one who corresponded with Jerome and sometimes argued with him vigorously. On the interpretation of Malachi, however, they were of one mind. We remember him as St. Augustine of Hippo, and he'll be a good place to wind up our survey. With St. Augustine, the theology of the Western Catholic Church is reaching its maturity.

CHAPTER 10

AUGUSTINE

THERE'S NO THEOLOGIAN more famous or more influential in the West than Augustine of Hippo. The story of his conversion, the *Confessions,* is one of the most famous Christian books outside the Bible itself, and simply taken as literature, it's a masterpiece. Many critics would say it's the first real autobiography: Augustine writes not just the events of his life but even more about the inner workings of his own soul. No one ever subjected himself to a more merciless self-examination.

Augustine was raised in North Africa by a Christian mother and a pagan father. His education prepared him to be a teacher of rhetoric, which could make him a comfortable living in those days. Religiously, though, he was an explorer. He spent a long time among the Manicheans, a sort of Gnostic sect who believed that the evil material world was always at war with the good spiritual world. Only after much searching—and many prayers from his mother—did Augustine find his way into the Christian Church.

But once he was in the Church, Augustine flourished.

He used all the resources his classical education had given him. Before there even was a Renaissance, he was a Renaissance man: in a wide variety of fields he became an expert, with his treatise on music becoming the basis of musical education for centuries to come. But his biggest influence would be as a theologian. He became bishop of Hippo, a city near Carthage in Africa, and already in his lifetime he was sought out as one of the most important thinkers in the Church. Leaving volume after volume of writing, every Western theologian since his time—both Catholic and Protestant—owes a lot to Augustine.

By the time we get to Augustine, Christians are so familiar with the Malachi prophecy that Augustine simply takes it for granted. Of *course* the Eucharist is the offering Malachi was talking about. Who could doubt it? Augustine seldom even has to mention it. But when he's preaching to a group of new Christians who have just been baptized, he thinks they ought to hear about it. They have never before shared in the Eucharist, but now they're about to do it. So he gives them what amounts to a summary of what all the Christian writers before him have said about the Eucharist: this is the pure sacrifice foretold by Malachi. The sacrifices in Jerusalem were images of the greater sacrifice to come, but this is the one that is offered all over the world, as Malachi said it would be. This is a *pure* sacrifice, so there is no bloody victim, because our great High Priest offered himself as the victim, and what you are about to partake of is his body and blood.

> You have all just now been born again of water and the spirit, and can see that food and drink upon this table of the Lord in a new light, and receive it with

a fresh love and piety, so I am obliged by the duty I have of giving you a sermon and by the anxious care by which I have given you birth, that Christ might be formed in you, to remind you infants of what the meaning is of such a great and divine sacrament, such a splendid and noble medicine, such a pure and simple sacrifice, which is not offered now just in the one earthly city of Jerusalem, nor into that tabernacle which was constructed by Moses, nor in the temple built by Solomon. These were just "shadows of things to come" (see Colossians 2:17). But "from the rising of the sun to its setting," it is offered as the prophets foretold, and as a sacrifice of praise to God, according to the grace of the New Testament. No longer is a victim sought from the flocks for a blood sacrifice, nor is a sheep or goat any more led to the divine altars, but now the sacrifice of our time is the body and blood of the priest himself. About him, indeed, it was foretold long ago in the Psalms, "You are a priest forever according to the order of Melchizedek." That Melchizedek, priest of God the most high, offered bread and wine when he blessed our father Abraham, we gather from reading about it in the book of Genesis.[1]

All of the Old Testament points forward to the Christian Church, offering its pure oblation from the rising of the sun to its setting.

---

[1] Augustine, *Sermon* 228B.1, in *Works of Saint Augustine*, vol. 3, bk. 6 (New Rochelle, NY: New City Press, 1993), 261.

But of course this means that the people who still cling to the Old Covenant are missing the boat. The fullness of salvation is in the Christian Church. Augustine believed that the Old Covenant was no longer in force, and that meant that people who still followed Jewish tradition no longer had anything to show for it.

> Now look for a prophet among the Jews; you find none. . . . You look among them for the faith of Christ; you do not find it. You look for a prophet; you do not find one. You look for a sacrifice; you do not find one. You look for a temple; you do not find one.
>
> Why is this? Because of the wickedness of those who dwell in it. See how he resists the proud! Hear how he gives grace to the humble! "He turns a desert into pools of water, a parched land into springs of water. And there he lets the hungry dwell . . ." (Psalm 107:35–36). Because to Him it was said, "You are a priest for ever after the order of Melchizedek" (Psalm 110:4).
>
> For you look for a sacrifice among the Jews; you have none after the order of Aaron. You look for one after the order of Melchizedek; you do not find it among them. But through the whole world it is celebrated in the Church. From the rising of the sun to its setting the name of the Lord is praised.[2]

While the quotation is not exact, it's obvious. *Where will*

---

[2] Augustine, *Expositions on the Psalms* 107.8.

you find the fulfillment of Malachi's prophecy? Augustine asks. *Among the Christians*, he answers. *You will not find it anywhere in Jewish practice.*

And this is because of the wickedness of the people who still follow the old law. We can see how this would be a big problem later on. Augustine is the most famous theologian in the Western Church. Everything he said was authoritative. And here he is calling the Jews wicked.

So what excuse does he have? Only the same one as St. John Chrysostom. He wasn't really arguing with the Jews: he was arguing with the Judaizing Christians, who were still a force to be reckoned with, though their numbers were small in comparison with the main branch of Christianity. Remember, again, that Augustine is preaching to a Christian audience. He must feel that there's a real danger of their falling under the spell of Jewish ideas. That must mean that they're closely associating with the Jewish community.

The argument also comes up in Augustine's massive *City of God*, which he wrote in response to the sack of Rome by barbarians in the year 410. Pagans argued that Rome had fallen because the pagan sacrifices were no longer offered. Augustine countered that the earthly city was temporary; the real dwelling of the faithful is the City of God. In the course of showing that the rise of Christianity was inevitable, predicted by both Hebrew and pagan prophets, Augustine finds time to open up the argument with the Jews again:

> Malachi, foretelling the Church which we now behold propagated through Christ, says quite openly to the Jews, in the person of God, "I have no pleasure in you, and I will not accept a gift at your hand. For

from the rising even to the setting of the sun, my name is great among the nations; and in every place sacrifice shall be made, and a pure oblation shall be offered to my name: for my name shall be great among the nations, says the Lord." Since we can already see this sacrifice offered to God in every place, from the rising of the sun to its setting, through Christ's priesthood after the order of Melchizedek, while the Jews—to whom it was said, "I have no pleasure in you, neither will I accept a gift at your hand"—cannot deny that their sacrifice has ceased, why do they still look for another Christ, when they read this in the prophecy, and see the thing fulfilled that could not be fulfilled except through him?[3]

To Augustine it seems completely obvious that Malachi was talking about the sacrifice of the Christians. Why would anyone think otherwise?

These arguments were really aimed at Christians, who were the only people in the audience. They were not very convincing to the few Jews who heard them. An admiring article in the *Jewish Encyclopedia* (1903 edition) praises Augustine's intellectual accomplishments, but doesn't think much of his arguments against the Jews:

His endeavor to prove the Messianic character of Jesus from Psalms xliv., xlviii., and lxx. is very far-fetched; as well as his plea for the rejection of the Jews, based on Isaiah ii. and Mal. i. 10, 11. . . . The

---

[3] Augustine, *City of God* 18.35.

results of such polemics—which, however, belong to the weakest and least important productions of his pen—were, of course, quite inconsiderable. Jewish natural intelligence sufficed to warn them against such conceptions of Scripture."[4]

. . . .

However, the prophecy of Malachi isn't useful only for arguing with the Jews and the Judaizers. It's a key that opens up the whole plan of salvation. It explains parts of the Gospel that would otherwise be obscure. For example, what did Jesus mean when he said, "Father . . . glorify your Son that the Son may glorify you" (see John 17:1)?

But since he not only said, "Father, glorify your Son," but likewise added, "that the Son may glorify you," it is worth asking how it was that the Son glorified the Father. After all, the eternal glory of the Father was never diminished in any human form, and it could not be increased in respect of its own divine perfection.

True, in itself, the glory of the Father could neither be diminished nor enlarged; but it was doubtless less among men when God was known only in Judea, and children were not yet praising the name of the Lord *from the rising of the sun to its setting.* But since this was made to happen by the gospel

[4] *Jewish Encyclopedia*, vol. 2 (New York: Funk & Wagnalls, 1903), s.v. "Augustine."

of Christ—namely, that the Father became known through the Son to the Gentiles—the Son certainly also glorified the Father.

If the Son, however, had only died, and not risen again, he would without doubt neither have been glorified by the Father, nor have glorified the Father. But now, having been glorified through his resurrection by the Father, he glorifies the Father by the preaching of His resurrection. For this is disclosed by the very order of the words: "Glorify," he says, "your Son, that the Son may glorify you"; saying, in other words, "Raise me up again, that by me you may become known to all the world."[5]

That is, what Jesus is praying for—and at the same time bringing about—is that the prophecy of Malachi should be fulfilled. It can't happen until the Son is glorified.

. . . .

Like generations of Christians before him, St. Augustine also sees the prophecy of Malachi as one of the most important proof texts of Christianity. You *know* the Christians are right, because the prophets foresaw the Christian era so clearly all those centuries ago. And no one saw more clearly than Malachi.

Augustine's example is instructive—we have to remember that he himself was a convert. Christianity was dominant in the world of the Roman Empire, but a large number of

---

[5] Augustine, *Tractates on the Gospel of John* 105.1.

intellectuals were still pagan. In fact, pagan tradition was still the basis of education. Augustine's mother—we know her as St. Monica—was a Christian who prayed every day for her son's conversion and lived long enough to see it with her own eyes. But his father, Patricius, remained a pagan, like a lot of well-to-do intellectuals. (Patricius converted only shortly before his death.) And Augustine had the best education he could get, which meant that he was exposed to the rusty remnants of pagan thought in the formative years of his youth.

Augustine's world was really a lot like ours. America is a predominantly Christian nation, but authentic-Christian university professors can be hard to find.

So when Augustine says that the proof from prophecy—and especially the proof from Malachi—is convincing, maybe he knows what he's talking about. Actually, he says that the proof from prophecy is the way to convince *pagans.* He's not talking about Jews or heretical Christians, who accept the Old Testament as inspired Scripture; he's talking about convincing the people who would seem least likely to be convinced by some old Hebrew prophet:

> For it is from prophecy that we convince pagans who contradict us.
>
> "Who is Christ?" says the pagan. We reply, "He whom the prophets foretold." "What prophets?" he asks. We quote Isaiah, Daniel, Jeremiah, and other holy prophets: we tell him that they came long before Christ, and how long before the coming of Christ they lived; then we make this reply: "Prophets came before Him, and they foretold His coming." . . .

And he urges: "You have forged these for yourselves. You have seen these things come to pass, and have written them in whatever books you pleased, as if their coming had been predicted."

Here in opposition to pagan enemies the witness of other enemies offers itself. We produce books written by the Jews, and reply: Doubtless both you and they are enemies of our faith. Hence they are scattered among the nations, that we may convince one class of enemies by another. Let the book of Isaiah be produced by the Jews, and let us see if it is not there we read, "He was led as a sheep to be slaughtered, and as a lamb before his shearer was dumb, so he opened not his mouth. In humility his judgment was taken away; by his bruises we are healed. All we as sheep went astray, and he was delivered up for our sins." (See Isaiah 53:5–8.)

Behold one lamp. Let us bring out another. Let the psalm be opened, and from there, too, let the foretold suffering of Christ be quoted: "They pierced my hands and my feet, they counted all my bones: but they considered me and gazed upon me, they parted my garments among them, and upon my vesture they cast the lot. My praise is with you; in the great assembly will I confess to you. All the ends of the earth shall be reminded, and be converted to the Lord: all countries of the nations shall worship in His sight; for the kingdom is the Lord's, and He shall have dominion over the nations." (See Psalm 22.)

Let the one enemy blush, for it is the other enemy that gives me the book. But look—out of the book produced by the one enemy, I have vanquished the other.

And do not let that enemy who brought out the book for me be left standing. Let him bring out that by which himself also may be vanquished. I read another prophet, and I find the Lord speaking to the Jews: I have no pleasure in you, says the Lord, nor will I accept sacrifice at your hands: for from the rising of the sun even to his going down, a pure sacrifice is offered to my name" (Malachi 1:10–11). You, O Jew, do not come to a pure sacrifice. I prove you impure.[6]

Like the earliest Christians, Augustine is still using the proof from prophecy to convince pagans. But it's hundreds of years since the coming of Christ by now, and the pagans themselves have the luxury of ignorance. They aren't automatically aware anymore that the prophets the Christians are quoting were actually writing centuries before Christ. How do we know you guys didn't just make all this stuff up?

So we turn to the Jews, whose own traditions vouch for the antiquity of the Christian prophets. No one accuses the Jews of being pro-Christian, but they'll tell you that these prophets—their own prophets—are older than the time of Christ.

But isn't there a real danger in bringing up the Jewish perspective? It's true that the Jews believe in the same Old Testament prophets. But they don't interpret them the same

---

[6] Augustine, *Tractates on the Gospel of John* 7.

way. If you turn to the Jews to confirm that you haven't edited the ancient prophets, you also have to be ready to counter their arguments that what the prophets meant was something different.

That's why Malachi was still one of the favorite Old Testament texts for fourth- and fifth-century Christians. He seems to foresee the Christian Church with amazing clarity, but he also talks about God rejecting the Temple priesthood. To Augustine, the Jews who cling to the old ways and refuse to acknowledge that Jesus is the Christ are part of that condemnation.

Augustine takes delight in placing the Jews and the Pagans on opposite sides, as equal and opposite "opponents" of the Christian faith. But his own argument makes it clear that there's something radically different about the two relationships. Pagans share nothing with Christians: although we can presume that Christianity, the official religion of the Roman Empire, was too big and visible to ignore completely by this time, there's nothing in the pagan tradition that points to Christianity. But Jews and Christians are obviously two sides of the same coin; they're still family. "Enemies" they may be, but their argument is still a family argument, where they can't agree on their interpretations of the same prophets.

CHAPTER 11

THE TRIUMPH AND
THE TRAGEDY

IF YOU PICK UP A STANDARD Catholic theological textbook from the early 1900s, the Christian interpretation of Malachi 1:11 is presented as fact. One of them gives us a syllogism to prove that Malachi meant the Mass:

> According to the Catholic interpretation, the prophet here foretells the everlasting sacrifice of the New Dispensation. The Mass, in the words of the Tridentine Fathers, "is indeed that clean oblation, which cannot be defiled by any unworthiness or malice of those that offer [it]; which the Lord foretold by Malachias would be offered everywhere, clean to His name, which was to be great amongst the nations. . . ."
>
> Malachias in the passage quoted predicts two distinct events: (1) the abolition of all Levitical sacrifices, and (2) the institution of an entirely new sacrifice. The only new sacrifice that complies with the

terms of this prediction is the Mass. Consequently
Malachias foretold the Mass.[1]

This doesn't mean that Malachi himself saw an image of the Mass in your parish church. The French scholar
Théophane Chary explains that Malachi's vision encom-
passed more than the prophet himself could possibly have
understood:

> In its ultimate fulfillment, well beyond the expecta-
> tion of the prophet, it is evidently the Holy Sacrifice
> of the Mass that is the outcome of this oracle. But
> in the primary literal sense, the views of the prophet
> are less complete and precise. He must necessarily
> have glimpsed the future through the facts of the
> present.[2]

Malachi looked at the future and saw no more sacrifices
at the Temple. Instead, the whole world was making a pure
offering to the God of Israel. And that's what we do, Christians have always said. To us, this pure offering is obviously
the Eucharist; this is the way Christians have read Malachi
from at least the *Didache* on.

But if what we took away from all this was that Christianity had *abolished* the sacrifices of the Law, we'd be making
a big mistake—and a potentially terrible one. Over and over

---

[1] Joseph Pohle, *The Sacraments: A Dogmatic Treatise*, vol. 1, *The Sacraments in General, Baptism, Confirmation* (St. Louis, MO: B. Herder,
1917), 296.
[2] Théophane Chary, *Les Prophètes et le Culte à partir de l'Exil* (Paris:
Desclee, 1957), 185.

the Fathers tell us what Christ himself told us: Christ came not to *abolish* the sacrificial system of Israel but to *fulfill* it.

As the New Testament tells us more than once, Christ's is the once-for-all sacrifice. That sacrifice is *consummated* on the cross, but Jesus actually makes the *offering* at the Last Supper. That's where he establishes what St. Thomas Aquinas would call the "newer rites of grace" as his memorial.

What does he offer? In signs, a "body" separated from its "blood." It's a priestly and sacrificial action that reminds us of the Temple liturgy. The New Testament vocabulary associated with this rite—*offering, memorial, communion*—is largely drawn from the language of sacrifice. And this dimension of the liturgy is what dominates the thought of the earliest Fathers, especially Clement of Rome, Ignatius of Antioch, Irenaeus, and Cyprian.

The American biblical scholar Scott Hahn has often said that Christ's Passion on earth is an image of the Son's eternal offering of himself in love to the Father. Theologians say that any small movement of Jesus' will during his earthly ministry would have been grace enough to redeem the world. But his whole life is taken up (and, as he put it, laid down) in his self-offering at the first Eucharist. He was laying down his life for his friends.

And our lives, in communion with his, are laid down on the altar in every Mass. Everything we do on earth—work, family, leisure—is taken up in the sacrifice. This is enacted symbolically through the rite.

But it's not *just* symbolic. The sign stands for a reality. "I am the living bread which came down from heaven; if any one eats of this bread, he will live forever; and the bread which I shall give for the life of the world is my flesh" (John

6:51). Jesus refused to leave the purely symbolic interpretation open: "For my flesh is food indeed, and my blood is drink indeed. He who eats my flesh and drinks my blood abides in me, and I in him" (John 6:55–56).

Why would it be such a terrible mistake to miss the point that Jesus fulfilled rather than abolished the sacrifices of the Law?

It would be bad because it would miss Jesus' own interpretation of his saving work: "And beginning with Moses and all the prophets, he interpreted to them in all the scriptures the things concerning himself" (Luke 24:27). For Jesus, the "scriptures"—what we call the Old Testament—were all pointing forward to his sacrifice.

Furthermore, it would render the Old Testament irrelevant at best and perhaps even false or misleading. We might even come to the conclusion that the God of the Old Testament, who wanted all those bloody sacrifices, was a different God entirely, whose concerns had nothing at all to do with what Jesus taught. Exactly that idea came up very early in the history of Christianity, most famously taught by a man named Marcion. This man told his followers that the God of the Old Testament was a wicked and inferior deity, and Jesus had come to earth to free us from his tyranny and introduce us to the previously unknown good God. It was the wicked Old Testament God who had created the universe, which meant that everything in it was evil. You can see how that would lead us badly astray.

Worst of all, thinking Jesus meant to abolish rather than fulfill the Old Testament sacrifices can lead us into one of the worst temptations Christians can face—the temptation to imagine that Christianity is anti-Jewish. The message of

Christianity is that salvation has come to the whole world. But salvation has come from the Jews. Christianity is right because the covenant with Israel was right. It was what prepared the world to receive the salvation Jesus Christ brought. Christianity makes no sense without the long history of Israel.

Family feuds are often bitter, and Christians and Jews are one family. We have an important disagreement about one important question: whether the messianic age is now or yet to come. But, just like in most family discrepancies, the terms of the argument make no sense to someone outside the family. The very fact that we disagree about this thing that makes no sense to outsiders shows that we are one people.

When we forget this identity, terrible things can happen.

That's why, even if for no other reason, it's essential to remember that Christ did not abolish the Old Testament sacrifices. What happened was what Malachi and the other prophets had foreseen hundreds of years earlier: in the age of the Messiah, the nations would recognize the God of Israel, and instead of the imperfect sacrifices offered at the Temple, one pure sacrifice would be offered around the world, from the rising of the sun to its setting. The Temple sacrifices would fade away—not because they were abolished but because their purpose had finally been fulfilled in a perfect way.

· · · · · · ·

The prophecy still strikes every Christian reader who comes across it. Catholics can't help seeing the Eucharist in Malachi's vision. And they're right to see it there. It would hardly be too much to say that you can't be a Catholic Christian without seeing the Eucharist in Malachi 1:11.

So we still see that one verse from Malachi whenever Catholics are writing about the Eucharist.

Take for example *The Eucharist in the Primitive Church*, by Edward J. Kilmartin—a Jesuit professor who was writing in the mid-1960s, right at the time of Vatican II. Malachi is at the very beginning of his book:

> It is unlikely that the prophet had in mind a form of worship existing at the time either among the pagans or Jews of the diaspora. The characteristics of this new sacrifice, its purity and universality, make it improbable that he was thinking of any sacrificial practice then in use. Consequently, Malachi announces a new, true, and proper sacrifice which will belong to the people of the Messianic age. In a vague way he looks forward to the sacrifice of the cross and its ritual representation, the Eucharist, which in the full light of New Testament revelation appears as the fulfillment of this prophecy.[3]

At about the same time, Father Eugene H. Maly was writing a book about the prophets of the Old Testament. He ends with Malachi, as the Old Testament does, and he points out that Malachi 1:11 "is familiar to all who have studied their Catholic catechisms" (at least it was in the mid-1960s). "It is presented, usually, as a clear prediction of the sacrifice of the Mass and hence as proof that the Mass was foreseen

---

[3] Edward J. Kilmartin, SJ, *The Eucharist in the Primitive Church* (Englewood Cliffs, NJ: Prentice-Hall, 1965), 4.

by Israel's prophets and willed by God."[4]

That little word "usually" might set us up to expect some argument that the passage isn't really about that at all. But that's not where Fr. Maly is going: "Unfortunately the presentation frequently neglects entirely the context in which the passage is found and the historical background of its formulation. When we study that context and background we shall see how amazing the statement really is."[5]

Fr. Maly is one of those who interpret Malachi as speaking of the pagan sacrifices of his own time—but as "a foreshadowing of a perfect sacrifice that would one day truly be offered 'from the rising of the sun, even to its setting,' that is, everywhere in the world." When we understand the background of Jewish nationalism Malachi comes from, Fr. Maly says, "This is surely a tremendous statement coming from the mouth of a Jewish writer."[6] Malachi didn't foresee the Eucharist in all its details the way Christians celebrate it, but he did see a time when all the nations of the world—not just the Jews—would be offering a pure sacrifice to the God of the Jews, not like the polluted one the Jerusalem priests offered in his own time. And that was something you never would have expected from a Jewish nationalist.

· · · · · · ·

Thus, if we say that John or Justin or Tertullian was anti-Semitic, then Malachi or Hosea or Jeremiah was an-

[4] Eugene H. Maly, *Prophets of Salvation* (New York: Herder and Herder, 1967), 185.
[5] Maly, *Prophets of Salvation*, 185.
[6] Maly, *Prophets of Salvation*, 185.

ti-Semitic. It's the same prophetic condemnation, the same vigorous argument about the outer observance and the inner heart. There's just one new thing added. For the Old Testament prophets, the messianic age—when all those abuses the prophets railed against would disappear—was somewhere in the future. For Christians, it's now.

Christianity doesn't make sense without its Jewish background. Modern Judaism doesn't make sense without its reaction against Christianity. Christians and Jews define each other.

But that same closeness that makes our arguments so bitter can also overcome the bitterness. We can start to work toward understanding each other—if we actually understand our shared history.

Christians can only work at the problem from our side, of course. First of all we have to understand why the centuries of vile things certain Christians have done to Jews might leave Jewish readers feeling queasy when they read the invective in some of the Church Fathers. Never mind that racism against Jews is a later phenomenon: the fact is that the racists adopted the language of the Fathers wholeheartedly and enthusiastically.

This explains how many Jewish readers feel when they see even the names of some of the early Christian writers. And when they see them writing about the "accursed Jews," about how "the Jews were disinherited" by God, how can they help thinking about ghettos and pogroms?

Once we understand that, the next thing is to remember not to apologize for being Christian. We feel sincerely sorry whenever people have done wicked things in the name of Christ. But that is not Christianity. If we apologize for being Christian, we're sorry for exactly the wrong thing.

To be a Christian means to believe that the whole of the Old Testament—from creation to Malachi, the last of the prophets—is pointing forward to the central event in history, the coming of the Christ. That means the Law and the prophets are images of the more glorious reality to come.

This, of course, is not something Jewish readers could ever agree with. If they believed it, they would be Christians. And if we Christians believed that the Law of Moses was the final word on what God's people are supposed to be doing, we'd be Jews, not Christians.

Furthermore, it's not just dishonest to pretend that we have no disagreement; it's insulting. Such guise suggests that we think our Jewish relations can't be trusted to behave like grownups, to have a civil discussion about our opposing views. No one wants to be treated that way.

But there's a right way to deal with the disparity. It's to be very sure of what we believe and to be able to explain it clearly if someone asks.

So what *do* we believe?

We believe that the prophet Malachi saw a vision more glorious than he could have comprehended.

We believe that the pure offering he saw represents the Eucharist, the one perfect sacrifice offered for all time by Jesus Christ, as it's offered every day in countless parishes all over the world, from the rising of the sun to its setting.

We believe that all the sacrifices of the Old Testament looked forward to this one perfect sacrifice, and that our sacrifice fulfills all those Old Testament images.

For from the rising of the sun to its setting my name is great among the nations, and in every place incense is offered to my name, and a pure offering; for my name is great among the nations, says the LORD of hosts.